Pleasure &

Suffering

By: Khushal Zafar

Chapters:

4

Preface:

This book should be seen as a thought experiment to investigate society. It should be noted that this book has many contradictions, but that is intentionally part of the story, as the story is meant to depict modern society, which branches into a plethora of many complicated facets- and this inevitably leads to contradiction. For, look at society and you shall see it as a contradiction to our very own nature, yet it somehow stems from our nature- that point itself being a contradiction. Furthermore, that is also one of the main philosophical points expressed in the book- showing through story format (for it is easier to explain in the concrete elaboration of a story, than in abstraction) the concept of paradox (and this includes the many contradictions of society). This paradox being something very real, yet in its nature hard to comprehend and furthermore, profoundly found in society and in all walks of life. To truly understand the concept of paradox, one must keep in mind that this book is a constant paradox- just like society- so that when your interpretations are brought into fruition, you shall realize there are infinite possible interpretations to the story as a whole and in each of their constituent philosophical phrases, concepts and parts (whatever you determine to be the separator of each philosophy from the other shall determine the different philosophical parts you shall arrive at through your own intuition). Yet all these infinite interpretations should be amassed into one single, ultimate interpretation: the paradox of contemporary society.

And that concluding remark to this preface too is in itself unironically a paradox- how fitting. And if this perhaps doesn't make sense to you at all, that is precisely the point of a paradox and this book should not necessarily be taken simply as the philosophy based upon the observations of society, but rather also can be viewed as a case study for understanding the concept of paradox and too the combinations of the two shall fit into understanding the ultimate philosophy, of the mind, life and reality. In the most simplest terms, I shall simply like to justify all complexities of my thoughts into a more concise statement, and yet of course this abridged statement does subdue my full intentions, yet to help derive the main point from the elaborations of my thoughts that make up the preface, I shall state in finality before you begin your journey upon this text; the concise statement being: the philosophy of this book is up to your interpretations and is completely subjective and therefore the book is written in the manner it is written in.

Furthermore, it should be understood that the characters represent archetypes- an exaggerated ideal, rare in absolute form in reality, yet all people in society have somewhat of each archetype in them, thus the archetype should be seen as a condensed version of societal behavior which acts in reality. Thus we rarely meet Lassie and Curt, yet we always meet a bit of them on a daily basis. Moreon, these archetypes can be considered metaphors in a manner and metaphors are often unconscious realizations that have not become conscious yet.

This book is very rude and crude and should be appreciated in a purely scientific sense, where all is meant theoretically and not as an absolute philosophy void of major uncertainties. In the end, the multiple endings should also be representational of the minute size of the philosophical mechanisms depicted here as a factor of societal functioning- however also note that minute factors too are often major in the end behavior of a civilization and thus what all this means, is that there is no concrete interpretation to any of the major philosophies of this story and to have any interpretation of this book is indeed ridiculous and necessary at the same time- a problem which makes me, the writer, utterly despicable, but yet at the same time an effective illustrator of society, for society in itself is oversaturated by uncertainty.

8

Warning: No philosophy should be taken as truthful- this book is simply a thought experiment within a fictitious world. I would think it psychologically dangerous to take many of the philosophies depicted from this work as truthful!

Daddy! Daddy!

"Daddy! Daddy! I want a puppy."

And it was with these simple words that our story begins, for these are the words of Lassie, the typical brat from those modern 'aristocratic' households composed of a precious angel, a voluptuous yet handsome maiden and a capitalist. None successful, yet none poor. And how many houses like these occupy the streets of our society? For this is no ordinary family, but rather a representation... this type of family is so common, so average that the only thing they are good at is being mediocre. This is the typical middle class family that for some odd reason thinks themselves rich- and rightly so, for they lack everything but money, yet they perceive themselves to lack money, for they lack contentment too. But like all good fathers, Mr. Rodriguez was not rich enough in intelligence to see any flaws in his beloved little angel. And like all good daughters, his beloved little angel was intelligent in seducing her father into getting her anything she wanted. In fact, that was the only thing she was intelligent in: vanity. For all the sluttiest of girls are experts in the appearance of innocence. And with a look of such innocence and childish guile that warmed her fathers heart, how could her 'daddy' not stop everything and anything and march towards the pet store... but no! Not the pet store, for remember, our dear Lassie was the mistress of vanity- she had to make all her actions brag-worthy, in the most innocent of manners- by means which made her appear a saint. And by such unconscious thought, she took her father by her Gucci gloves and Balenciaga slippers to the shelter. And the deed was done!

Now ego and vanity are two intermingled concepts and as I had already told you, Lassie was an absolute idiot in all matters but vanity- it appeared as though by her tender age of 14 she had specialized so heavily in it that perhaps all her mental efforts had forgotten about anything else. If a man were to jump off her ego and land on her IQ, he would fall so long that he would finally think he was flying. But even in Lassie's case, he would hit the cement and die, simply like all who took the blunderous plunder into her life. She was not evil, neither did she think much of herself. However it was her over obsession of her image- she would never be at ease until the whole of humanity thought she was an utter perfection. This was her ego- an ego so large and insecure that it had consumed her wholly into the slavery of other peoples opinions. And perhaps this had occurred due to her magnificent stupidity. Or perhaps her stupidity arose from her magnificent insecurity. But nevertheless, this is vanity! Oh vanity! Oh vanity! How destructive you are...

For Lassie was not intentionally evil, yet her vain stupidity was so wretched, so problematic and worst of all, to her non-existent. It was as if her soul and the devil had secretly betrothed. This was Lassie.

Lassie too was one of those girls who wanted to be maternal. She appreciated things cute and had this desire of child- yet she was not conscious of her wantonness of being a mother, yet it manifested itself in her high sex drive- and by that I dont mean an act of pleasure, I mean a full personality emboddied her, where she had that sweetness of a mother in her, which was far from unarousing. In the psychological world, one can appreciate it animalistically, as signals, perhaps even feramoneious signals which penetrate the skulls to let one know that she is to be courted. Lassie too was one of those girls who was high-maintenance and had too much comfort in a warm house, where her biggest problem was whether she would wear rouge de le pomme lipstick or scarlet macaw lipgloss to match the underbelly of her Louboutins on her evenings out. And in such safety, boredom and maternal desire had arrived her new puppy and she named him: Sparkles.

Childhood

As Lassie was the joy of the house and Sparkles was the joy of
Lassie, Sparkles too became the joy of the house. Sparkles was
pampered, loved and cared for like a child...a human child. It
was endless, unconditional affection. Sparkles was taken around
everywhere, body wrapped by a purse, head cloaked by smiles,
as he cruised around licking the open air that swathed through
his black and brown hair, returning much kisses and care. All
of Lassie's friends stroked Sparkles and granted him presents of
wet lipstick, or even fighted and defended him in times where
he had exercised his more animalistic side. He was so
pampered, he might as well have been wearing pampers.
It is of great importance to understand how a dog grows up in a
loving house- for the dog becomes human to a large degree.

"Sparkles... oh, Sparkles! Look what I have got for you."
"Oh Sparkles... Oh sparkles! Come give me a kiss."
"Oh sparkles... Oh Sparkles! Lets play."
"Oh sparkles... Oh sparkles! Lets go for a walk."
And Sparkles, had bones with the marrow, every day in the
morrow. And sparkles, was always in company of either Lassie,
the mother, or even the common tickle by Mr.Rodriguez. And
Sparkles, sat every night on the lap of Lassie, as she did her

work. And sparkles would always be invited out with Lassie, sitting in her purse by the doggy treats, with his cheeks pinched every few minutes, in the adorned affection of his mother, dear Lassie, who talked in her cute baby voice, cuddling him. And she would talk to him about her day- despite the difference in language, Sparkles still understood her emotions and watched as she would, days on end, have excitement, or would sullen in the need of his comfort, as poor Lassie, only in her early years of high school was discovering the disastrous pains of life. Such so, Sparkles would often look at her tears and think that the world had turned out to be a lie and luckily, he didn't understand her words, thus, he could sleep in that peaceful ignorance of being able to innocently pity her circumstances; and it was lucky sparkles didn't understand Lassie, as thus, Lassie could be honest and shameless in the truths of her insidious emotions over such utterly underwhelming issues, that she did often feel heard and better. Yet, let us cut her some slack- for the teenage years are always difficult- it is the years a human learns to be inhuman, which unfortunately most people never unlearn and thus totally remain inhuman for the rest of their lives. And we may joke about this young Lassie, yet, we mustn't forget that perhaps people are simply forgeries of their environment and thus, when we find a Lassie in every highschool, we know that society has suffocated upon the filth of the collective ideology of the modern world. And so, we may even say, we look at animals and children and notice they are natural, yet, look at adults and pets and see they have become distorted in their nature. But alas, don't strain your eyes, for we shall see this more in due time. All one needs to know for now, is the callings of the household were constantly a mingle of affection over sparkles- a very distinguished, young gentlemen, much respected and loved in society, with his cute cheeks, droopy tongue, sleepy, yet playful eyes and tipsy bark. And lo and behold, a dog looks for nothing more than the simple love of his name and a kiss,

"Sparkles... oh, Sparkles! Look what I have got for you."

"Oh Sparkles... Oh sparkles! Come give me a kiss."

"Oh sparkles... Oh Sparkles! Lets play."

"Oh sparkles... Oh sparkles! Lets go for a walk."

And happily he slept, in the peace of affection that every being looks for. Atleast, every being enslaved by society, that is, for in the wild...

Yet, that's not the point. Lets just end it here and say: Sparkles was given great affection.

Note: when a surplus of affection is given, it is even meaner to take that affection away, then if that affection was never given in the first place and perhaps that is what people fear, when they are given affection and find themselves insecure- for how often does one find themselves disturbed by affection, compliments or simply even the idea of being loved. And also, what does one think of being brought up without love, is it not then that people sometimes feel incapable of love? Well have we not got a paradox here?

Simple Gaieties

Simple gaieties are simply the finest joys for those who have not yet been plastified.

Oh simple gaieties. How sweet you are.

The warmth of the fireplace. The sweetness of the snow. The smile. The hug. The affection.

Oh simple gaieties. How sweet you are.

How sweet it is to be cradled in a purse.

Petted by friends. Talked to.

Oh simple gaieties. How sweet you are.

And in play, one runs and barks and chases.

One harasses and is harassed, not in malice, but in benevolence.

And one is kissed, fed and bathed.

One is taken for walks and adventures.

But most of all. One is given attention.

Those are simple gaieties. So simple, yet sometimes so rare. And it is the acknowledgement of this melancholy fact that too is bittersweet like cinnamon or peppermint. But are these not the finest pleasures?

Oh simple gaieties. How sweet you are.

But oh simple gaieties, how time deforms!

For it is sad that now man doesn't appreciate these simple gaieties.

For it is sad that man often doesn't receive these simple gaieties.

For it is sad that simplicity is no longer considered a gaiety.

Oh simple gaieties. Have you been lost?

Lost with the time?

But oh simple gaieties? Where have you gone?

Oh! Has the world forgotten about love?

Have you been replaced with status?

Oh! Simple Gaieties. Come back! Come back!

For my grandfather used to say: "the good old times."

For those were the times of simple gaieties.

But my good friend, where have you gone?

Have you disappeared like the rest of my friends?

Like my other friends, have you gone to chase your ego?

Have you become tired of yourself?

Have you gone to become fancy?

Oh no! I see it now. You are no longer simple gaieties! You are fancy pleasures.

Oh no! I wish to pierce my eyes, for you are ugly! Ugly!

You fancy pleasures, you are a delusion.

You fancy pleasures, you make us gamble.

You fancy pleasures, you play with our emotions. We are high and then we are low. You are no joy, you are exclusive, raw pleasure. You do not last, you are illusive.
You fancy pleasures. Go back. Go back. Bring me my old friend!
You fancy pleasures, you never satisfy me. You provoke me. You seduce me. Yet, you are no joy, you are only pleasure!
And often when one advances towards pleasure, do they not advance away from joy?
For you fancy pleasures- you have advanced. You fancy pleasures, you are hideous, yet you wear the mask of beauty.
You fancy pleasures, you shall be the ruin of people. The ruin of society. The ruin of earth.

Ah, and fancy pleasures laughed, kissed Sparkles and ascended to the house.
Sparkles woke from his nightmare in a cold shiver and although the fireplace still was warm and comforting, his bed still soft and fluffy, he knew that fancy pleasures had introduced himself for a reason.

Sparkles let out a spur of breath, sprawled back onto his bed, absorbing the comfort of it all, smiled and whispered, "oh simple gaieties. How sweet you are."

...Time...

As the mascline sands of time, slither, trickle and tick through that feminine shaped glass... wait... is that not the perfect analogy for nature of reality- where orderly time is warped by the chaos of that feminine expression that we call: "life." And is it not time that seems so straight, so endlessly running, yet is always so elusive in our reflections? Is time not a funny subject? For when we look at time, do we not feel scared, lonely, melancholy and anxious; romantic, ecstatic, dangerous and gorgeous? For time... ha... time is that unreal thing, that is somehow real. And indeed this unreal thing, really did end up moving along and began its aging process upon our heroes- the family and our villain: poor old sparkles. As of our current temporal positioning, we find sparkles to have resided at the Rodriguez residence for little more than six months, yet as time loves to deceive, this seemingly short while, is also seemingly a long time. Is six months not too short to forget about a newborn? Is six months not too long to remember a new toy? And as we have it, this was exactly the position sparkles was in- not remembered, yet, not forgotten. But even in this short period, a long story has been formed. For, let us firstly understand this story before we continue. For, even though six months is such a short period of time for a life to mature, sparkles had matured... matured too much for his own good.

On the eve of the adoption, sparkles had been received in the most pomp manner, with such tender love, such affection, such lustful eyes glided upon him- in such a luxury, one may become pretentious to the ideas of ideal love- of ever happiness- perhaps even utopia- yet for we know from history, utopias are always dystopian, just like unicorns are always dragons in disguise. Sparkles was shown off to all of Lassie's friends. She would take him everywhere, cradled in the warmth of her heat and between the lips of her purse.

Yet, now, we see something different. Sparkles has no longer received the affection he is used to. Sparkles, no longer chews bones in the morning, sparkles no longer gets treats, and sparkles no longer gets touched by the neither the mother, nor Mr.Rodriguez and often Sparkles is only given attention when Lassie desires it, yet when sparkles whims for it, he is left down to drown in his loneliness. Sometimes, he is lucky to be able to sit by Lassie on the sofa as she watches a movie, yet, at other times, he is told to go away. And is this not the worst kind of pain- the hot and cold games of the most teenage romance- or shall I say immature, for how often does one see the same behavior in adults? But worse than anything, is that it isn't intentional games- there is no underlying desire behind it, a desire to manipulate for the craving of someone, because no- Sparkles was no longer craved. No! Sparkles was simply a dog. Not a puppy. A dog. The family dog. And in high time, when Lassie was lonely, when she didn't have anyone else- she would come to him. And at first, it might have been so, that sparkles was lucky to not understand- but is the pain of being only a last resort not so unbearable that even animals grow conscious of it? And thus, Sparkles was conscious of it. But sparkles, a house dog... was a dog that had no other friends- a dog who didn't even have the opportunity to make friends. And here, thus, sparkles being starved of affection, could only but appreciate affection, no matter how backhanded it came, just as a man starved for a week, shall eat a rotten apple simply to be able to survive- for now sparkles had become conscious enough- human enough- to need the basic human need of affection. And so, here Sparkles lay, full well knowing his lack of desirousness, yet unable to move. And here, he too in his teenage years has learnt to no longer be natural. For he was never natural- he was a pet dog, bred by humans specifically to be weakened, to be joy tempered and then as if the distortions of his nature weren't enough, he was nurtured too to be a human, not just in birth, but too to learn the loneliness of teenagers. He was now in his teenage year- the years of heartbreak and the years where all humans, including sparkles, learn to leave behind nature and join the psychological machinery that some call civility- for that is the society we live in- a civil society and to that, one must declare that here lies the great problem of our minds: civility means becoming a person who abides by the culture of society, yet culture is corrupted by the arrogance of men and women.

The boyfriend

Like any good civil girl in her 15th year of age, she would have to have a boyfriend- for what good civil girl doesn't start engaging in fornication at this time? What a disgrace it would be for a woman to be a virgin at 16! And brace yourselves, for one might think that is ridiculous, but my dear readers- one must remember, we are not talking about every teenage girl, we are talking about the mentality of the Lassies' of the world. A mentality, so deranged, so focused upon the glam, which for some reason is given to early sex, yet so hidden, Lassie perceived herself to be but ready, fertile, maternal and in want of the joy, just as she perceives every boy to be overjoyous of her and thus, she desires not the boys who would like her, but rather the boy, who for some reason is not caring of her herself. The fundamental problem with the Lassies of this world, is that they are stupid. And not just stupid by a lack of mental functioning, but they have grown their stupidity from the seeds of their ego- the seeds that stave upon the idea that she must be better than everyone else- something which is know as that superiority complex- something theorized to cover up a deep rooted inferiority that they feel. And here so, a boy would love her- just as sparkles had loved her, yet, no... how could someone who loves me possibly be someone worthy of me? And thus, enters Curt . Alass a boy... a boy who sees nothing but sex, as a mingling of his pubescent desires. A boy who shall never love Lassie, but: who cares? ... for he makes her feel sexy and what is possibly better than that for the Lassies' of the world? Someone, who will boost her ego by his actions, yet who will also, make her feel the immense pain of hurt- for the only way that Lassies' can possibly feel that they are with someone of high status is if they are hurt by them. Only can they falsely build their ego, by first getting it torn down. And this is exactly what Curt does, whether he knows it or not- perhaps, he doesn't know, yet what he does know is that he wants sex and in all honesty, he knows he doesn't want love. Let us just note that, if you are to starve someone secretly, they will love you for giving them a piece of bread; if you secretly hurt a Lassies' ego, she shall love you for grabbing her ass. Sex makes her feel desired, while his lack of affection does the opposite. Such boys first eliminate a woman's sense of desirability, desecrating their ego, and thus, a woman shall, through her insecurity go to lengths to amend it and thus, here we have a player's tactics. And here too we see the dangers in such a society where vanity has become synonymous with civility. But the unfortunate thing is, that such insecurity plagues society all over the world... no wonder tears are bitter, for these Lassies' are far too many and these Lassies' never learn, and if they do, not until they are far too old. And thus, a man too becomes distrubed by the world, by the woman, by himself and thus, a many men change into beasts- loveless, lustful beasts. But yet, that is the nature of sex- for the great problem is that people have it without love and commitment and thus, it is nothing more than validation of vanity.

And too, here Sparkles was in a stage where unfortunately, his ego had been torn- yes a dog with an ego- what a monstrosity our society has made and then ripped apart. For every time it rains, perhaps nature is crying over the catastrophe of that machine known as society.

Curt

In such a state, Curt has entered the picture, with little love. He was the vile bastard* to have caused suffering onto young Lassie- a suffering which had started at her eyes and moved towards her heart- for at the heart it had become obsession. And from this obsession, Sparkles was nothing but a blockade to Lassie and thus in Lassie a great annoyance grew, for every moment Curt was with Sparkles, a jealousy grew, for she wanted him to pet her, not him. So she slowly grew angry with Sparkles. And Sparkles's attitude, always with his innocent socialization- that which he was deprived of, he would come at them, he was eager and Lassie, had finally concluded that this Sparkles was too clingy- too much in the way. Too annoying. And no Longer did she value sparkles, instead she detested him.

Why is the word bastard used to describe terrible people? Theory: Because a broken family so often produces a broken person. Bastard is a metaphor and metaphors are unconscious relizations.

You see, these two work in pairs. Lassie and Curt- two corruptions of society- yet, the fact that they are multiplying tells us that the unfortunate thing is, these two are becoming the new equilibrium in civil society. For these two are the easiest being to be- they follow one rule: vanity. Now we shall get back into the ideology of Curt's, yet at first, let us appreciate one thing. Despite the lack of love that Sparkles was receiving, in all irony, the one person who showed him the most affection was Curt. Now was this to make Lassie jealous, or was it simply a nicety, or was it that he liked dogs- or perhaps, he loved dogs, yet only liked Lassie's body? Perhaps, we are overthinking and perhaps, 'bird of a feather flock together'? But despite it all, one thing to know is that, Curt, without a single failure, had always given sparkles a rub on the head when he entered upon the house and to this, we have that ironic feeling, where Sparkles seemed to like Curt, yet... as we understand, there shall be an underlying drama, with that hideous confusion- for, as we shall see... jealousy is a harsh thing and for jealousy is very often the changer of men into Curts, unless a Curt is naturally formed through the circumstances of the heart, which many men have a burden so stifling, we are almost tempted to feel pity for these Curts, for these Curt's may be argued to be causations of their circumstances, yet- I will not be so disrespectful to the men who have toiled in their excessive pain, tempted at every step to turn into these Curts, yet, have remained decent. No I shan't pity these Curts. Neither shall I pity myself in my sorrows. For devastation has arisen in every corner of the world and despite personal pain, the really savage thing is the that this story is written through the observations of an unobservant writer, who somehow managed to understand the conspiracy of disgrace that has been assigned the code name: civility in contemporary society.

Curt II

What makes a teenage boy aggressive, abusive, self-centered, immoral?
Throughout his life, Curt had never fully comprehended love. He came from a rich family that consisted of a mother, and a younger brother; he did have a father, however he was absent in his life, for he was in that self-made penitentiary which is called: workaholism. This father was an entrepreneur, who left the house at 6am and returned at 10 pm, working 6 days a week. It had always been this way, since the day he was born. And so, Curt was the type of boy, who didn't perceive men to be affectionate, for he had never seen a man be affectionate throughout his childhood. He would often go days without seeing his father and are fathers not those who are to instill discipline upon their children- and so Curt was a boy who lacked discipline. His mother was sweet, yet was a woman who the boys stopped taking seriously and so, often the father would intervene in rage upon the boys when their mischief had reached too far. One profound memory that was seen throbbing about the skull of Curt was the time he had to be picked up by his father from the police station late in the night for shoplifting from the local corner store.

"Why? Why? Why would you do something like that? You have money, but still you decide to steal!"

And so, through this and many incidents like so, Curt subconsciously felt no love from his father and so, the liquor of rebellion seemed to brew. That fatherly love is of so great importance for these young boys, yet in its absence, plus the high ratio of aggression he had perceived from his father, he had never learnt the meaning of love. He had never understood the idea of a man to be able to express it. He had learned that men should be aggressive. And his father had a simple answer to everything: money. So Curt now believed that money was the answer to all problems. And it seemed that his mother was the same way, for she simply enjoyed the money, but lacked any great relationship. She took care of the kids, however, there were no family dinners, there were no family activities- it seemed that the habit never developed, for the father was never there and the unison of family always starts with the time between a mother and a father. But so, the mother often did her own thing- the boys did theirs and in such disconnect, there was loneliness upon each soul in the household. There were no family values. And so, Curt, was a boy, who had no conception of a family, a lack of education from his parents and so, he had only his animalistic desires.

So here we have it... Curt- a young boy, who doesn't know of love, who thinks money is the solution to all problems and a boy who feel oppressed by his father- feels weak in his presence, so in an overcompensation, begins to try and feel strong in other places- and here arises his abusive streak. And furthermore, because he has no family at home, he focuses his energy upon the people of school, his friends- yet that too with that underlying depression of fatherlessness- that underlying depression that further transforms into more aggressive energy via his conscious effort to feel adequate- to allow the ego some piece of not feeling like a failure, despite- to prevent himself from feeling like a loser- something ingrained within the depth of his psychic structure, due to his lack of belongingness- and so- these type of people are often the most popular in school, for due to their lack of true belongingness, they put dramatic energies into being socially acceptable- they put in profound efforts to have a value socially. It is often the fatherless that are extremely successful either socially or criminally.

But, there is no running away from the internal depths of the psyche, so thus, there is no running away from the deep seated insecurity- thus we have Curt- a corroded character. A character who feels abandoned and detached from people. A person unable to love and thus his desires are fully animalistic. And how many Curts are there today in society? Many!

Furthermore, as Curt had never been shown how to respect women from his father, nor even from his mother- he has little respect for women. More on, these Curts have just come, abruptly, out of the age of thinking women have cooties and that they are some lesser being into that confused age of puberty, where they are highly aroused and a girlfriend acts as in 2 ways to them: firstly as a status symbol; secondly, as a plaything for their sexual desires.

And so when a pretty girl like Lassie likes a boy and often Lassie likes the aggressive boys for they formulate the top of the the playground hierarchy and thus a boy like Curt who lacks any appreciation of love for girls, is vain and thus the combination of the two with his aggression, causes him to be an opportunistic megalomaniac- the exact type that are popular in highschool by the Lassies of the world and there you have it- an abusive boyfriend emerges, not responsible enough to even know the meaning of love. Arrogance, vanity, greed and sex dominate the ideologies of his life. And that is a Curt for you. And unfortunately it is a cycle that for many Lassies, likely fall in love with again... and again... and again. Some ponder upon this question: why? And there are perhaps many possibilities to the underlying reason behind this and we mustn't declare any to be the true reason, however some say that it is to overcome their failure of the first Curt they fell in love with- for the first relationship like this was a monster of a blow to the ego and thus, she must once again challenge this Curt and succeed to change him- for then she can rest assured that she is a woman. And perhaps one asks, why is it that women like Lassie want to change this man? Well, that is now another interesting question that we can only speculate on, but perhaps, it is because change is a feminine concept- it is a concept that when occurring in a man, is part of his feminine side and thus, a women being dominated by the feminine energies of the psyche, we can only imagine that change is so critical of a concept to a woman... but alas, I, a person of the male species, cannot comprehend the answer to this question and thus, retire upon it in acceptance of the uncertainty of it all. But perhaps, one may also ask: can a Curt be changed? Perhaps. But far too often it isn't the case and this often drives a woman into the fragile state of such a case. And perhaps it is subconscious too, so a woman doesn't even understand that she is messing with a Curt and this too is one of those statements which can lead to a profound matrix of questions and so... here we have the case of romance: a confusion. And so, Curt... oh fellow Curt... you despicable person you... but perhaps there is a bit of Curt in all men of contemporary society and perhaps thus lies the great tragedy of modern civilization.

One often hates how Curts' are rewarded for being terrible people and so how often is one rewarded for the deeds they commit that seems to defecate upon the concept of ethics. Oh tragic world we live in!

But note; the insecurity of the Curts' drive them to act mean, as they are enraged by their shortcomings and thus cover it up in, by producing a fiction of grandeur. It is a constant battle between the truth of reality and their idealized image that causes chaos in their souls and thus the abusive anger bubbles within the Curts' and the need for attention in the Lassies'. It is an internal torture that produces external destruction.

The Ego

The ego is a very specific function of the mind- it is the identification of the self- an identity. But identity is so grand a structure, so huge a concept, one mustn't simply say it by a singular word, but one must elaborate on it. It is in fact, so grand a thing we are talking about, where we shall refrain from calling it simply as 'identity', but shall properly refer to it as: ego. It is this ego, which occupies the central strata of the mind. And the mind is such a turbulent place. Chaos on all sides- a sphere of constant aurora. The mixing of lights, that erupt out of atomic combustion of particles, radiating cosmic energies: that is the mind. But here, within this dynamic sphere, sits a solid globe- changing still- yet still held stable enough for solidification of matter, yet still mostly liquid. It is this liquidity tho, and exactly this liquidity which makes it so compassionate to its design, for it reacts and moves, yet stays put upon the roundness. It flows and it suspends and it reacts and the atmosphere moves it- the atmosphere builds up mountainous waves, the crash and rupture- the sheer weight ripping through the stones that burst through the water. And it is heated and rises and then cools and coagulates into mist- mist which hugs tighter and tighter upon itself- mist which weightens itself and then, when the time is ripe, mist that falls- mist that soaks the grounds, the beaches, the plants- it circulates in all of life, this liquid, it flows down from the heights of mountains, where it sometimes freezes, sometimes not: yet it flows. Ebbs. And flows. Down into the valleys. Into the lakes. Into the rivers. It goes everywhere, yet, it still remains still. It remains on Earth. An when seen from afar up past the atmosphere, there it seems to seize its grand movements and their too, we may stand upon the distances of the galaxies of the mind- we may stand somewhere within the boundless unconscious that somehow runs from the ego into who knows where- for just like space- we don't know the furthest regions of the mind. And just like the earth, we don't know fully what lays in the deep cracks lining the ocean beds of the ego. And so, here we have the ego, two-thirds fluid, one-third solid, suspended somewhere within the great expanses of the mind.

Now that we know the material of the ego- the material is dynamic, yet relatively static. And which lay in the membrane of a reactive atmosphere, where the radiation of the unconscious interacts with, we also have one more proponent in the mix: The alien. And what is the alien? That green being who stands upon the distant galaxy. He is simply a far away observer, sitting upon the rocks of Jupiter, where he smokes a cigarette and watches as the ego produces a vast life of its own. It is just so, that this alien has nothing to do with us... it is just so that this alien teleports... it is just so that this alien is invisible to us- for this alien is simply that being who can be expressed as just another one of those weird phenomena that occurs in the abyss of the unconscious, which we simply have no possible idea to what it means, nor if we truly even ever get a glimmer of its existence- for that is the unconscious- a place where there is so much, yet so much more that we are unaware of. It takes great depths of understanding to build the rockets that venture into the unknown, yet still we have never found aliens- so, despite there being aliens within the mind, we still simply cannot do to think that we shall find them, when we cant find them outside.

But so, in this model, we still have to rendez-vous at one peculiar instance- something of nothing- something of everything. The radiation of the solar system. For there is a difference of radiation coming from our good friend the sun and the radiation coming from strange planets afar, is there not? And you should answer: of course there is! There is most definitely a difference. For one is explained clearly, the other, not even explained, if even picked up on. And so, we can now understand that the radiation coming from afar is that of the unconscious mind- very much seemingly random and perplex and much a mystery in its own rights, except for perhaps that little bit we do somehow understand through the mind-bending efforts of theoretics. But on the other hand, there is the intense radiation of the sun- that radiation, which sometimes when looked upon in pureness- when looked upon from outside the ego- that immensely powerful light- the light that in its pure form fries- that is the radiation of the senses. Yes. the five or six or seven senses- whatever the true number you perceive- it is that- the radiation of the sun is the senses. But of course, like the Earth, this radiation hits the surface of our ego, by passing through a membrane- that membrane being a dispersion of gasses, which are much natural and innate, yet, are also much dictated by the activities of the atmosphere. And so, it is this membrane on the ego, that is controlled by the ego- this membrane that filters the different radiations- allowing some to pass, while deflecting others away back into the unconscious. And Now let us develop our metaphor more- let us appreciate the ego, as a concoction of both conscious and subconscious functioning- and let us digress from perhaps the sensible ideas of what fluid and solid are like and do something that is perhaps the reverse of all psychological literature and say that the fluid is the conscious, while the solid is the subconscious- but why? For one simple reason. The fluid molds the solid. And so, the conscious mind is there to mold. But what about the ratio of solid to liquid in the ego? Let us ignore that, for we all know that consciousness, is rarely ever pure consciousness- within the ego, we have a plethora of simultaneous thoughts- it is just how we are able to construct metaphors and relate to taste- perhaps it is not so direct, but just so, Europe touches asia in multiple points. And so, we shan't take anything here as an absolute. Infact, here we shall end our metaphor of the ego, with one final iteration of perhaps that much too important concept: the radiation from the sun dictates much of the movement of the water, while the water constructs the ridges and paths of the solid- it forms the beds that turn into rivers- it formulates this all, into a continuous cycle which self- enhances itself more and more with the advance of time. And just so, we must ask, does the starting position of it all matter? Yes. Yes! Yes, ofcourse. If the first mountain was located 2 centimeters to the left of its original positions, the Athabasca River would be upside down! Yes and yes! It all matters. Of course it matters. And so, what is this thing that we are metamorphosing into the starting positions of the planet? It is: Childhood!

And so, now that we understand the origins of a child's behavior, we too know that the radiation shall too change the behavior of the ego, with its ripples upon the water, while it too expands and contracts the ground and too the direct influence of this radiation affects the subconscious part of the ego, where once again it is all forged into a path for consciousness. Yes indeed. But what is consciousness? Something which we cannot say we know, for we experience the world through our ego and the ego is a mix of that fluid consciousness and that solid subconscious, looking out into the world through the atmosphere- that same atmosphere that is dictated by the activities of the Earth. And so, again we must repeat, and I must say this repetition is a perfect illustration of the concept we repeat: the concept being: the cycle of the ego is a reinforcing feedback loop. We see through our ego- and that vision builds our ego, which we again see through, which once again, builds. But now, finally, after this iteration has been over, as I have promised, we shall stop with this wretched metaphor and express that the water is alive!

Because the water is consciousness. And so the water has the ability to move itself, to shape itself void of outside factors. Well, not fully void, for there is always radiation, but this consciousness is capable of fighting with the effects of that radiation and maneuvering itself in such a way as to restructure itself with its own thoughts. And so, that is what the water does- the water thinks and so thus these thoughts start to mold the ego from within. The ego is the surface of much reactions of different elements of the mind, which synthesize into thoughts, feelings, emotions. And thought- is thought not that great vortex of the mind? Somewhat of a black hole and thus I have spoken of not using the metaphor anymore, for, we cannot necessarily say that the blackhole is on Earth, or Earth is inside the blackhole- for perhaps logically we may answer, but in some wretched tale like this one, sometimes the thoughts become dark and descriptive in such a manner, that it seems that all the ego has ventured inside itself- thus placing a blackhole within the center of the Earth and in so doing so, the earth in itself is consumed by that whole- it is consumed by itself. That is Hysteria! Hysteria- when the emotional wrath of the mind so greatly exudes its gravity out, that the mind consumes itself into a never ending loop, where it keeps sucking itself within itself for perpetuity, for the black hole pulls evenly on all matter, pulling at it from all sides in never ending cycles of stretching round and round into the central point, where the gravity of it is so strong, that the whole construction of the universe collapses and thus does the hysteric man find himself in another galaxy, somewhere stretched out between multiple universes in that grand multiverse that scientists debate of: does the multiverse exist? And I shall answer: Yes it does! Yes, it indeed does exist. It exists in the potentiality of the mind: the potentiality for destruction.

And so now you understand what is meant by the ego. Why this simple statement of identity is simply accurate, but not accurate enough to arouse a true appreciation of the ego. And indeed, the ego is exactly that of identity- that is correct, but what is Identity? The ego is identity! Identity being that grand phenomenon. So grand. So powerful. It took black holes, planets, aliens, universes and the absurdity of metaphor to describe. That is what identity is. Of identity! And no wonder, so many a wars have been fought over identity. Why so many a people lose sanity from identity. Why Identity is of such great passion, that so often people completely lack any originality with their identity. For here springs identity: Identity!

And so identity dictates almost all the notions of our life- it dictates our whims and desires- our behaviors and actions- our visions external and internal- the interpretation of our visions- it filters our senses- it encapsulates all of life as we know it. Oh how does the color blue look to one or the other- different- for through identity we have different determinations of the world- some subconsciously- or in cases of synesthesia- consciously- taste sweetness in the color blue, while others taste saltiness in the color blue: for this is identity. Identity. The thing so grand. And so, too in identity, we have the rebellion or the conformity to the identity- both are those which change this ever-changing, static ego. And so, understand what identity is- understand what ego is. But mostly understand how all of life is brought about through the ego!

Vanity

The ego, being identity, is that which draws the boundaries between a person and the world- it identifies the self, as a separate entity to others. And so, what is vanity? Vanity, is the barricading of these boundaries into walls of stone- walls vast like a sort of intergalactic chinese wall. Something, which brings forth separateness and so with separateness comes loneliness. It is so complex a matter, to distinguish the mechanisms at play, so best to undertake such analysis by the ideology of love.

Oh love. When we are in love- we no longer say that we are separate beings- but use language like, "you complete me." "we are the same." A father tells his son, "you are an extension of me."

And so, with love, you see the intersection of egos- you see the boundaries breaking. You see connectedness. Yes. And so forth, we realize when we relax the ego, we poke holes in its plating- we feel at one with the universe. And so- that is love. That is therefore the rising issue of the ego. And despite the ego being unescapable in life- despite it being so necessary for beings- it still has its major tradeoff: the tradeoff of connection- sincere connection- the intersections of two people- the becoming one with the universe: love. Yes, it is so, that the ego is a mitigator of love. Those with strengthened walls- they don't love- for love requires the entering of one person into another, while they simultaneously enter you and so, there we see the connection between the ego and love- the necessity for the walls of it to have doors- perhaps vast doors, to allow the intersections. Now of course, we cannot leave all boundaries eliminated, for there must be some demarcation in order to understand the separateness between mental and physical bodies simply to be able to function in the world. And so, lines are necessary- yet must remain permeable to love- not simply in romance- but to love the world- to allow the world to enter- to allow nature to enter- the sceneries of the galaxies and the oceans and the sunsets and the people and the birds and the children. That love- that is only possible when there is weakness- for love is a weakness by definition. Only if a person allows themselves to be weak, is it possible for them to love. And thus it is only the exceptionally brave, who allow their borders to have pen doors. And so it requires extreme strength- it requires security within the kingdom to love. And so here, we come to the catastrophe which is vanity. Vanity- that great intangible force that runs through the ego and causes the waters to surge up and close the doors. It runs to the volcanos to overheat into steam, to close the atmosphere- it clouds the atmosphere- darkens. The clouds rush around. The cages are thrown on the town. It is vanity. What is vanity? Vanity is the exaggeration of the word: ME!

It is the protruding insecurity. It is this insecurity which occurs from a many possible places. As we have stated, there is the radiation from above- there is the childhood below, there is the thoughts and thinking, all which waver from wherever. There are memories. There are ideas. There is of course some great insecurity trying to be covered up- trying to be hid beneath the clouds. Or there is simply, distrust of the outside world. Or from which side of it all- there are many possible places- but where it comes from- let us forget that in its totality. Let us not dive into all the mechanisms of it all. But let us understand that it is vanity which runs red in our society. It is everywhere- it is injected into our brains by advertisements, by friends, by family, by schooling and of course the sum total of this is that it is a spice added to the ideology that modern civilization is based upon. In all truths, it is so toxic, that it is this vanity, that causes people to go into jobs they don't like, thus to say they are successful- but due to their hatred of their career, they find exactly nothing real to satisfy their internal desires and so cling more greatly onto that perceived success: that vanity.

The thing about teenagers is that they are fresh out of childhood. There is much to understand about their character, yet we can see that they are a direct representation of their neighborhood, firstly, their behavior stemming from their parents and family, then from their social circle at school. In the highschool year, it is the time when children learn the concept of identity and their brutal attempt to make their identity valuable is what often characterizes a growth in a dangerous direction. The teenage years when a child steps off the platform of innocence and begins walking the path of vanity.

It is of the 2 dimensions, a young boy's relationship to his parents and the development of his identity, which breeds the Curts' of the world. In so far, they are spoilt, but Vanity is a need to cover up the insecurities. Insecurities arise from the expectation that one must be of a certain nature, of some form a greatness, or cleverness, or richness, or in the teenage years: coolness. It is a sad realization that people too often don't realize the simple deception of the ego in man- that is that it is all a fiction designed to entertain the torrents that are innate in every man and woman who is too bored for their own good. Insecurities arise, by the minds' being empty in a manner that is unhealthy- for minds are meant to think and when lacking in constructive thoughts...

The secret to being freed of the notion of insecurity is to realize how absolutely nothing we are as human beings- how insignificant. For insecurities arise from trying to be a significant character- a perfect character- but that is an impossibility, for us humans are naturally imperfect- and perhaps that is a means of perfection- for it may be the imperfections that make something perfect, like scratchy paint, known dearly by antiquers as vintage patina. But alas, perhaps that is the whole idea of vintage patina; perhaps that is the whole idea behind such beauty in imperfections, it symbolizes ourselves: humans. And what are us humans? The definition- extremely imperfect beings.

Thus, here we have it... insecure, for we think we must be perfect and this idea is chartered within us in our teenage years- some unfortunately realize the great folly in this ideology, yet with great despair one realizes that it so often is accelerated by the masses of such classes of society. One can easily identify a vastly contemporary mental disorder by the defining symptom: their chief hobby is to observe celebrities.

The Defense of Vanity

So... Vanity.

That thing we so disgust. But perhaps we have excessive disgust for it?

We have excessive disgust to it for it is that destruction of self we so dearly need. For the only way to escape it is to escape all forms of socialization, but we are social animals. And so... we desire to look good for ourselves and others. Which is the beginning of vanity. But then... we look for the borders of where to be vain and where not to be. And that is where we become confused. U know, it's funny. They say, just be yourself. But... who is yourself? Are we not different with different people... or in different moods? And then... is there really such a thing as the self? And so... then... if there is no real self? Are we just... a mosaic of vain ideas?

So... Vanity.

There is nothing so natural in attracting a mate as vanity. There is nothing so vain as physics- for even solids deceive. We perceive something heavy and full to be thoroughly dense, when in actuality, it is empty. And we perceive things to have form, when it so is that all particles are energetic dispositions and forces at play with our puny minds, by the irrational emotions of nature. And yet so, we become absorbed more and more into the paralysis of understanding existence and fiction. We are so consumed by our attempts to understand reality, we forget everything is nothing; nothing is everything; all existence is inexistence in this curious concoction that we swim in. So such is the paradox of trying to understand: we try to delineate everything into separations and categories, for that is the mechanisms of language; language is the mechanisms of our thoughts. And so we are sometimes unable to answer certain questions, for we are unable to ascertain the true meaning behind these questions. So thus... where does thou draweth thy lines between vanity and reality? And thus, where does one dare to say that someone is being vain and where one is showing you their inner truth? And for so looking into where one mimics perfection, can thy not say it is indeed perfection that mimics inferiority? And so, nature might be seen as vain... yet... nature perhaps is not vain, only our thoughts about vanity, being so outrageously unnatural and insufficient a conception of reality, can be thought of as vain. As descartes states, "I think, therefore I am", perhaps, here too, we can state that perhaps, "I think of vanity, therefore there is vanity." But alas, that too is such a bleak conception of thoughts, it cannot be considered truthful, but rather a vain facade, of the underlying reality. So then... what is vanity? Where can we draw the lines?

Is this a problem of human nature or society? Once again we must ask whether human nature and society are the same: does societal nature stem from the innate nature of humans?

Abandoned

Is confusion not the most painful emotion?
Sparkles now lay in the sand, between the bushes, in that weak
state of overthinking which only a human is capable of. It was
here where a sad reminiscence broke through his senses. The
scene was obscene- not physically, but emotionally, for it didn't
make any sense.

Sparkles had been cradled in Lassie's arms, that loving action
which he hadn't felt since he was just a child. In that delicate
dance, where he lay in her arms, she meandered about in the
night and finally lay him on a bed of grass, gave him one last
pat on the forehead and just left. She said ofcourse in a soft
voice, "don't worry, we shall see each other often, " as a
crocodile tear slithered down her cheek, yet had sparkles
understood this? Not just the words, but the tragedy of it all?
At first no, but now it has become apparent.

Sparkles had of course went after her, however, she simply told
him to stay, so he did, expecting her to be back. And like all
home-kept dogs, he sat with that doggish smile, where his
tongue drewled upon his chin, with excitement panthing bout

his face. Yet, he sat and sat, until his posture had tired... where was Lassie? She had not returned.

At first, Sparkles had worried for a day or two and ran all over the place in his gullible innocence, thinking that Lassie was in trouble, yet he had soon seen her entering one of those fancy mercedez of a boy he had never seen before, however as he ran to them, she had closed the door, a moment of eye contact had occurred and then she turned her face...

"Had I done anything wrong?" Sparkles couldn't think of anything! "Is it my fault she left me?"

And while we talk about confusion, let's ask: is confusion not the greatest pain? The greatest melancholy. So hard, you don't feel sad, even though you wish to cry, yet... you can't, for you are simply draped in the chasm of confusion. Woe to such a place!

It is the simplest actions which are often the most painful, the most confusing- not what the actions mean, but that perpetually terrifying question of: why?

And often people don't realize how important the closure of this question is to ease the heart, and how cruel it is for one to abandon and never give the solace of reply to such a question. And how dreadfully easy it is to ponder upon this question for all of infinity, for every theory is a hydra, where one head chopped off, sprouts three anew. And to make it worse, had she not cried when she had told sparkles that they shall meet again? And how much a disaster it is to uncover a lie- to see beyond the facade that someone you loved, someone you thought you knew, someone who you thought was good- and find that all of them was a fiction... for if they were all a fiction, what of you is real? If all your care, all your compliments were fake, then what of me is real? What of me did you actually appreciate? What of me is of any value? And so goes the ego, rampaging through its identity crisis. And ofcourse, although sparkles didn't know this, dogs don't have egos. However, sparkles had drunk the poison of consciousness- that poison which developed into the ulcerous tumor known in modern medicine as: the ego. He developed it all from Lassie. For a dog naturally cares about his worth- a dog is simply a dog- and that is what gives nature so much power, for nature is a spontaneous operation, unlike us humans who have perverted our behavior with such ridiculous thoughts, wondering over things which have no answers. But yes, he was given the ability to grieve and then was made to grieve by the same person who had declared that she had loved him- the same person who had been Sparkles's only mother, for he had been separated from his true mother, for the pleasure of his pseudo mother. And now it was the same person who had abandoned him- without any emotional support, not even an answer. And even harsher to it all, is how little she even recognizes what she did, how little does she even recognize the pain of Sparkles. Sometimes all we need is to be acknowledged- we need our emotions acknowledged, but no. Not for Sparkles. What a common tragedy it is. How often are dogs bred inferior to their nature for human pleasure? How often are dogs ripped from their mothers, for human pleasure? How often are dogs abandoned due to human displeasure? How often (never) are dogs given an answer for their abandonment. And worst of all, how dare we make dogs conscious of our human emotions!

For after years of brainwashing into subservience, he had finally concluded: since I have been abandoned, then who can I belong to?

Now the dictum was set. And so through the set of emotions, through the set of conditions, through the set of outcomes, Sparkles now set off to settle into his new life, into his new identity as: The Lonely Dog.

The Children

At the corner of the block, there lay a patch of tall bushes that made up the address of the lonely dog and now in fine time, many children would address him, for he was their new toy. In such moments, where the Sparkles had been granted that loving affection, he found such profound joy and excitement, such the type that a girl like Lassie found over buying a new dress. Here he would lick and dress the children with his arduous energy. The children would sometimes come with food and for the first week upon their discovery of him, he hadn't had to hunt at all, yet was given of all sorts of delicacies for a dog, such as fat chopping, meat and bones. More so, he now had friends. Every time he would see a child, he would run to meet him and so too would the child run to him- the mood these days was like a constant summer hymn, below the bleating sun and the marching winds of March. And upon the course sands under the stalks of rose bushes and that single palm that sprouted, Sparkles watched the course of the moon stalk the stars as it would rise and fall upon the planes of the palm of the sky all the way till fall- for he was satisfied and only in satisfaction can one be so calmly meditative in their mindless observations to see beauty without those logical reservations of thought. Indeed, is it not perfect to be mindless?- to lay calm in the breeze- to see calm into the night sky- to rise calmly with the sun- to be calm in all its manner, is what monks and sages have been trying to figure out for ages. And here, Sparkles, for he was at such moments: Sparkles. And is it not of the greatest elation to be able to have an identity- for humans of contemporary society all seek identity. And here, lay sparkles all summer, juxtaposed between the comfort of his old identity and the past calamity- for, does a passing depression not always amplify the boon? And so here too, Sparkles, had tasted the bitterness of desertion, rejection and emotional slavery and had now been freed of it and thus the affection, attention and respect had the excitement of novelty, yet at the same time, it had the warm nostalgia of childhood. You see, humans have a sixth sense- the sense to reminisce back to childhood and due to this, people's behavior is often greatly modeled over their childhood experience and through such return of this feeling, Sparkles now slept in that cute tiredness, that all puppies have due to the sheer exhaustion of their tragically difficult lives. And thus, so Sparkles slumbered calmly.

The Blue Baboon

On the other side of town, a cafe called the Blue Baboon, stood with two stories; the top of the cafe had a veranda, laced with old mahogany, which under it lay a table out looking onto the melow sea. There was a blue gloom in the sky, as a light condensation drizzled. As night approached, one could see the street lights streaking upon the damp ground, animated by the quivers of the light rain. Each puddle glimmered in such excitement, bursting with the colors of yellow, white and the tints of the neon that radiated from the cafe.

It was dark out, yet, still, not fully. From the balcony you could see far into the horizon and would notice the slight tint of napalm rays that stroked the clouds. If you looked to the left, you could see the city upon the sea, and too, to the right you had the docks. Yet when u looked straight, you had the reflections of it all upon the water. Yes the water... What a perfect metaphor. For all the lights of the world were reflected in such psychedelic proportions, riffled by the waves of the black unconscious known as the sea- if you stared at the water, you understood Van Gho, for in the reflection of such a distorted medium could you look about seeing the world with that utter realization of distortion that illuminates the mind into wonder. And ponder upon the lights of the finals rays of the sun, as they

creeped up from the horizon, to the sandy shores, while mixing with the exoticism of the illumination from the city and the smokey calm of the port, where a sailor or two chatted away about their catch over a cigarette, while another man weaved the nets and lines, preparing for tomorrow's expedition.
Yes and in so fine a moment, a smooth bluesy jazz was bussing in the cafe... perhaps a philosophical jazz... for that was the mood of such a cafe and here upon that table at the edge of the veranda that we had spoken of earlier- here sat two men in their early twenties sipping their coffee in observation of the world, yet it is sometimes often that when a man looks out into the distance, he also looks deep within.

"You know... the other day, I saw a fox catch a rabbit and for a moment, I almost felt bad for it, but then I thought... well, hell. That's life. Innit?"

"Bro. I'll tell you something. Something which hurts, yet it is one of those rational pains due to some sort of perhaps... irrational circumstances."
"Aight. Go for it."
"There is this dog. Abandoned on the streets by my place. And I'll tell you. I feel for him. He has become lonely. At first the children would play with him, but he has become a nuisance.

He is always running to them... and you know it scares the kids, for now he is a big dog."

"Well. That's just how it goes. Innit?"

"I'll tell you. I use to pet it. I would play with it, every once in a while. But you know, I did something yesterday... something which... well, lets say im not happy about.

You see, every time i'm out, he keeps running up to me and he jumps on me. Im on my way somewhere and he comes filthy as the streets and jumps upon me. So... that's it I thought. I was on my way out and he ran to me, but I had lost my patience and at him I stamped.

Oh. I remember his face. He was shocked. He seemed betrayed. And he seemed sad."

"Sad. A dog? You're A crazy boy."

"Nah. I saw it. He felt betrayed. But it's like... what can I do? But still. I felt so cold."

"Well. You did nothing wrong. Is that not the nature of life."

"Oh dear. Have some sympathy. He has been abandoned! He is left nothing! And yet, to be honest, what can I do?"

"Oh. Do know me. I can relate...oh I can relate. For I identify with the dog. It is the unfortunate conditions of reality. You know, it reminds me... I had once fallen in love with a lesbian. I still remember it. For what a disaster that was. For what... I felt so rejected... devastated... lonely... for that is the heart my dear friend. Like the rabbit and the fox... life eats you up. And I know exactly what the dog feels, for he may even feel pathetic. But my dear friend... that's life. Oh life... only when you can accept pessimism can you finally be optimistic. And thus, I would advise your good friend Mr.Doggo to stop having emotions. But alas, it's hard..."

"Oh I'll remember that."

"And remember... don't take it too serious. Don't take embarrassment. Don't think too much... for everyone feels pathetic when they try. And oh... sometimes we don't even know... and sometimes... we can't help ourselves... and sometimes we try to make things better, but only make it all worse. Sometimes, you even try to be friends and realize you are jealous of all her friends, for you realize she doesn't even see you as a friend, but you feel for her and you worst of all... you realize you mean nothing to her whatsoever. Oh! Even if it wasn't anything, you atleast want to be around her... for... for you enjoy her company... for you love her. For you would do anything for her... and thus a man even eventually tried to leave her alone... but... oh! How can a man not follow his heart..."

"I see this is no longer about the dog."

"No you see it is. For I am that dog!" And a tear started to lubricate his eyes, as he looked down in embarrassment. "I am the dog, who after everything got stamped. And I am the dog, who got abandoned. I am the lonely dog. For we were friends...

good friends! And now, ever since I confessed to her, and I know I shouldn't have done that, but alas, I just did… It happened. And only then was it revealed to me that she was gay. Only then did I realize how stupid I was. And then if only she could just accept the compliment. But no… everything evaporated. You see I only told her because I tried everything else and this pain… it was killing me… the pain of her not knowing, for I had hope and when there is hope it forces you to face the greatest risks of all. And alas. At that moment, it was as if we were never friends. And okay… I tried to be friends with her again. And her response was… don't worry, you didn't ruin our friendship… but it was a lie. A LIE! For since that moment, for 3 months, I felt like that dog. Always chasing, yet always stamped. I felt unwanted. I felt as if she looked down upon me. I felt… well… what could I even do? But alas… huh. Just don't say I should have sympathy for this lonely dog… for who has sympathy for themselves? I am that lonely dog. And surprize surprize… it hurts. But that is the unfortunate irony of life: there are often no right options! And alas… leave us lonely dogs without your pity… for we have enough loathing for our pathetic selves."
A moment of silence lingered, as they both sippes their coffee and then he began again, "it's hard to be a good person. Oh how I had thought such ridiculous things. How I had wanted to hate her… how I had wanted to even hurt her… but alas… that is life, when u expect to fly, you simply fall. Oh so. I retired to tears

and introversion and still... I do feel the pain... but I have accepted this as a tragic romance and so... so too will the dog... for remember, he is a dog- only humans have the capacity to become corrupt, for it takes a certain level of intelligence to be an effective villain. Stupid villains are just known as 'nice guys'."

"But those nice guys you speak of are never actually nice."

"No. They're nice- but not good. For being good is a pain... a pain indeed and perhaps the worst kind is when you are mistaken for weakness or meanness for actually doing the thing that is hardest to do. And for all the wrong judgements that people often have on those who are struggling in the constant conflict between good and evil. For remember, being just is often the opposite of being nice. Not just just to other people but just to yourself. And here you have the paradox of the lonely dog! You were just to yourself by denying the dog. And that's simply life... ah life. How often does a man become ruined by rejection... through rejection does a man often turn into a monster... and thus, it's best to remember: that's life, a constant battle to be good through rejections. And that's simply life... ah, life."

" I saw a fox catch a rabbit the other day and I almost felt bad. But then I thought: that's life."

"Exactly."

And they both smiled in that bittersweet appreciation and looked out upon the night. For... that is the sad realization everyone must have, yet no one wants to have: Oh. Thats life!.

The acceptance of solitude

As the lonely dog meandered through life, he sobbed as his array of dejection grew. He had met a cat... but no, cats don't hang with dogs and so, he hadn't found a compadre with the cat. And he had met an owl in the night, but alas... no luck there, for owls are solitary creatures.
And finally he met a fox, but to keep up with the fox... haha... impossible, for this fantastic little fox was always running and always getting into mischief and no matter how much the lonely dog tried, he just couldn't be friends with the fox.
And upon the wild dogs, he was able to communicate, yet he simply couldn't understand them, for the lonely dog was all too human. And the wild dogs seemed to be weary of him, for he wasnt of their pack. But they finally concluded he was a harmless idiot and so too they let him be, they even let him hang. But they were too busy... they were always on their operation for food, or for whatever wild dogs do... the lonely dog simply couldn't understand their strange world so found company, but no... no friendship. And in his lonely misery he still strolled the streets looking for acceptance.
"Ah a rat! How exciting." Sparkles thought as he littered the bin as he buffeted upon the scraps and roaches.
"Eek!" It yelped as it dashed away.

"Am I so hideous? That no one wants to be around me? Ah. The raccoons hiss at me. The rats screech and dash. And the dogs ignore me." And upon his thought, he finally asked the age old question of terror" "who am I?"

Like a human in the modern machine of society, this dog soon knew everyone, but knew no one. And for that is our progression of society, yet still we wish to progress further.

And the lonely dog lingered in the night, perusing the streets in search- search of what? He no longer knew, but in search of something- perhaps solace or contentment? Perhaps his identity? Perhaps in search of himself? Perhaps...?
And as he stepped upon the puddles in the tipsy-lit streets every night, he searched and searched with no avail, but alas he arrived at sort of solitary peace for the moments his memories died and his life of love and childhood no longer haunted him... those were the fine moments he appreciated the present and in such moments the concept of time dissipated into a far away land. Such moments were those when he licked at the puddles and watched as the reflection shattered and a surge of patterns erupted into his eyes. And upon such moments he sat in his trip as the beams would swirl off the waves and pop designs into his eyes. It was a grand amusement, for experiencing seemingly

unimportant such things always are. It is rather a breathtaking
exercise for it questioned his understanding of metaphysics...
for these patterns that resonated from the water didn't seem to
exist as objects, they didn't seem to be held upon the water, but
rather produced by the eyes... a sort of hypnotic illusion.
And sometimes as the lonely dog licked the streams that led to
the gutters, he met some crickets, yet like the rains of fall, they
would fall away as he approached and once again the lonely dog
became lonely. It was after months and many tries that in the
end he accepted his condition and retired his ambitions and
began to see the world as a lonely enterprise for him. Perhaps
this is an example of what the Buddhists say, "desire is the root
of all suffering."

The solitary dog

As introverts have been saying from time immemorial, "isn't solitude beautiful." And so the lonely dog now became the solitary dog. And with this new found identity, life became musical- more musical than ever before. Time by yourself- calm yet exotic- like the nights of the light. Ah, now the solitary dog strode upon the street in his full contentment. And is it not in solitude where you truly never feel lonely? For solitude is the time of discovery- a time to look out into the world, upon the open stars and observe- not just see- but experience an observation, to feel sensual with your surroundings, to think, to introspect, to tug on the creative faculties of your mind.... Oh solitude: how sweet you are.

And are not extroverts funny- for they constantly chase the folly of socialization, as if socialization can possibly ease the mind of their inner desire to live. But alas, in other people we are constantly avoiding the archetypal drama that is to play in our psyche- that drama which is ever so important to the realization of man to himself. And so, we look at the animals so balanced in their behavior, for they have already realized themselves, only in the overly complex society man has constructed through his fallacious logic do beings lay that are unrealized to themselves in their natural proponent and thus they concoct all sorts of theories to somehow achieve their holism or better yet, they are socialized into an idea which often spreads like the plague. But some may argue that this is inevitable, for that was the poison of the apple. The apple! The apple that had kicked us out of heaven. And perhaps they are right, perhaps not... I can't claim to know, however what I can claim is that if my observations are honest to me, it appears that man is far too confused upon his own condition.

We too often see the arrogance of ideologies displayed in the mediums of their latest media, for example the hypocrite capitalists- my favorite being the wanna-be entrepreneurs and the men who preach of social hierarchy as if it is the one truly philosophy, for cringing is sometimes important to stretch the face. But in all times, there is an importance to the observation of these different ideologies, for it is the mixed understanding of a matrix of ideologies that allows one to truly grasp the complex concept of any matter that is born upon the world. Infact, I find it of utmost important a realization that the clearest sign of an intelligent and educated person is their capacity to understand uncertainty and thus, is the modern concept of confidence- a view that confidence is to be certain- really just a sign that a man lacks intelligence. For I must declare, in my view confidence has become a vague word that means nothing, for if one were to look at it they shall see that nothing of confident action is ever actually done with

confidence, but due to some other underlying mechanism which gives the appearance of confidence, such as experience, a well constructed plan, an act or deception carefully designed to imitate a model, or even a lack of thinking- for sometimes stupidity is indeed a producer of this so called confidence.
Oh and here perhaps are the thought of a philosopher dog- a dog who sits in solitude upon a rock upon a cliff upon a starry night and upon such a time looks out into the vastness of space and so too does he look out upon the vastness of the space within. But no. This philosopher dog is not the same solitary dog, for all those great simple gaieties come to destruction by fancy pleasures and it is unfortunate that by the evilness of me, the writer, I must express to you that the solitary dog didn't stay the solitary dog long enough to become a great philosopher or even to realize himself... no, for that would end the story without having me depicted all I wish for you to see and so here strolled sparkles upon the ridges of the valley that ran perpendicular to that little town of his when he saw her: The White Bitch.

The White Bitch

Through the bushes and shrubs upon the cliffs, the solitary dog footed the grounds as he sensed his surroundings. He smelt the fall peppermint that grew wild and along with the berries and the last of the white lavender. And in such an environment, he ruffled through the bushes and so too he heard another roughling and thought, "what could that be? For it was too loud to be an opossum, yet lacked the violent stillness of the raccoon."

And it grew nearer and nearer and soon he found himself orienting himself towards its path and thus she had arrived, delicate and dainty, yet mischievously smiling in jolly. Yet there she stopped, her head peeking out behind a berry bush, half covered and there she lay looking at the lonely dog and the lonely dog stood staring at her.

And for the lonely dog didnt know what to do, he continued with his glance for as long as she looked upon him and as time started rolling he felt his pupils dilate and warmth running through his veins as a meek fuzziness began to enshroud his vision as time began to slow in that beguiling moments of incomprehensibly fantastic observations.

Her coat was white and elegant all over, and seemed to reflect the light of the moon more so than the moon reflected that of the sun. And in the dim light they stood there he noticed her cheeks were chiseled and tapered gently, and had such a delicate complexion, with such playful danteurs upon her lips that cusped a woolfish snout. Upon her snout lingered thin black nostrils, that were not dry, but certainly not droopy and at the end their lieth her eyes. Dark eyes. Deep eyes. Eyes that so well contradicted her fair coat- that was so pure white- even the most emphasis wouldn't be able to fully describe the angelus glow it radiates. And those eyes... oh those eyes, they twinkled, they shined, they glimmered... and those eyes, the lonely dog saw something in them, he saw all of life, he saw dreams, he saw soulish depth... he thought he saw her soul... he saw a person.... Not just a being, but the whole of a person... down into the core, such glorious play in those eyes! Such a being! Oh, for her eyes now rupture the facade of his skin and she saw into him, she understood him, she connected with him intimately. And with that, she smiled at him, winked, turned back into the bushes and then trodded away.

And so simply does one fall in love for the first time and once again he had hope, he had aspiration and thus he exhaled, which cleared his head and alas he realized he should catch her and so he ran after her, but where was she? He searched for a brief moment, until he started feeling awkward and that brief moment of heat had turned into a dizzying melancholy, where his legs were shaking, his heart was racing and so his mood grew vermillion with love and rosy with the opium of optimism. Huh, he exhaled in quivors and began panting as he sat down. And slowly... but no... then quickly, with each beat of his now slowed, yet thick heart, he felt the power of serotonin pulsing through his arteries and artilleries, numbing his veins into that blissful euphoria, as the vision started to grow... oh the innocent vision of a child's first love... how sad it is that society has made it almost a certainty that it shall be a disaster, for is contemporary society not a hater of love? Does contemporary society not try and block out love as much as possible- leaving it a punishment for which two people fall in love are given argumentations and laments of the stupidity of their hearts. And how is it that love is now becoming for the older and older, for oh... how do they not realize it... love is stupid... and it should be... love is for the children, for children are natural and for as we mature we lose our innate stupidity- that beautiful stupidity slips away by the chlorox of society bleaching our minds to anything that defiles their capitalistic or prejudiced or vain logic. That same logic that respects intelligence is also that same logic which eradicates that beautiful stupidity that is simply so critical to the development of intelligence- for you must live! You must live in passion to be intelligent! What intelligence can possibly be produced through boredom? And is logic not the crux of the bored philosophy- for it is emotion that adds the spice to life and so they destroyed love for the young and thus the only thing left to feel was hate. But let's stop here! For we are not to apply human corruption to nature- for nature remains natural... marvellously stupid and thus infinitely more intelligent than us puny humans.

And so here we have it... the beauty of youth; the beauty of a first love...

The Gangster Dogs

Now the lonely dog strode through the meadows and the streets with bliss of that vision: the vision of love. The profound picture … that most powerful archetype of some profound psychic story!

As the lonely dog reached the corner of the park and rifled across the forest, there laid an underpass in the dawn breeze, where now two dogs barked quietly in the vexed confabulations of banter. As The Lonely Dog passed by he bellowed a rowdy, "howdy," and then stopped his feet, yet his energy still carried away in that searching spirit that bestows itself upon the searcher of heartly entanglement that he was now trying to bond with. It is that same flushing energy that makes one incapable of staying in one place long… for that is the nature of the courtly horse that gallops in at its will, busting open the gates of that castle of glass known as the heart. Here the lonely dog didnt know whether to stay or to run, or to gallop, or chitter chatter in some banter, nor did he know of what it was that had approached him, for love by definition is that intoxication that stupefies a man into the blissful stupidity of simplicity- the simplicity of the logical mind. The only complexity left, is the complexity of the heart, which is the psychic structure that finds no ailments in such profound depths- it is only when the mind starts to comprehend the passions of the heart that a person feels overwhelmed in that exhausted anxiety that is too often wrongfully symbolized by a blue heart. No no. At such a moment, for such a simple creature... the lonely dog was veiled in the warm passion of love.

And with such elation as enwrapped by the chemicals of love, a man so easily and so often becomes an extrovert... an open extrovert....opened up by that optimism that like heroine mustn't be abandoned, for else... Love like any drug is dangerous.

And as the lonely dog now stopped under the overpass, amongst the two black dogs, little did he understand their nature... but at least they replied:

"Haha... howdy."

"Haha... what's happening."

"Yeah... u up pretty early to be chirpy and ah... we seem to see ya loosely around town."

"I haven't slept all night. I'm simply too joyous to sleep!"

"Aha I see... I see... I mean, if you have some catnip, y'all might wanna share."

"What? Catnip?"

"Ahh I see... he tryna hide his stash."

"Nah nah... he prolly found some of them liquor in the bin... look at him... he warm as a pumpkin in the fall winds while us two fools here standin under the overpass sober as an eagle."

"Damn eagles... never know how to have fun. I tell you... I tell you, next time I see that punk who stole my rabbit, imma show him... you watch... we gonna eat him and his momma... damn eagle."

"Yeah... word of advice, never leave your meat unguarded or those damn, no good, thinkin-they-smarter-than-you hawks gonna squak your supper. Me and here my brother, we caught a rabbit and was gonna eat it for dinner and fine time we left it in a bush and what do u know... an eagle snatched it. Thats theft man... and then we have some hocus pocus bloke tryna tell us to save our meals for the winter."

"Well, hocus pocus, the joke is on us. We fools didn't even last a portion of the day."

"Nah nah. The joke is definitely not on us. He's the one going to be a sorry."

"The rascal was fooling, man. Imma tell you. He pullin our tails. Iva never seen him keep anything for more than a minute. Bloody boy doesnt even let his prey die before he consumes it. Greedy little dog."

"And man... there is that terrier up on May street. He always pullim some limbo on us too... u heard what he be a tellin me yesterday?"

"Nah. A what he sayin?"

"Man he was a tellin me that now they shipping dogs out to the navy. He said that now a dog is to learn how to use a machine gun and throw here grenades. I thought... that a pretty nifty thing to a do and went down to the local military office and nah... they didn't ask me for a paw print or here nothing... bloke looked at me like I came to beg for food. Man but little does he know I actually a came to make some fools begga me for their lives. That terrier... man... he a lucky I don't join the navy, for I woulda been shootin up old may street. Damn terriers."

"Listen a here boy... never trust a terrier. They always calling for some fiction. Always a terrier gonna say he flew a harrier or some of the likes... how? He cant even reach the controls... damn terriers."

The Lonely Dog stopped in a moment to gather what was happening. And as the two dogs continued their banter, he looked at them. They weren't old, but likely older than him, yet still they were quite obviously on the younger end of the spectrum. They were twins, both black, yet had slight, faded thin brown stripe that were perplexingly straight and ran down them in a manner that wasn't prominent, but rather noticeable gave them a strikingly aggressive look- the look of an imperfectly black coat- something street- something wild- something savage. They had thin long snouts and pointy ears and a jawline that matched. Their body too was thin and shredded, yet they wern't buff; everything about these twins seemed to be an aerodynamically designed feature. They were clearly light and their legs moved rapidly and often, even as they stood in the cold of the night chattering. If a Darwin were to see such dogs, he would have probably exclaimed: "oh! These dogs have evolved to race. And such energy! They must surely hunt the prairies."

And out of the background gossip came the fleeting question, just enough a remark that The Lonely Dog here understood, but just barely, for he was lost in the affairs of his mind, "and a what type of a dog are you?"

"I don't know…"

"Eh… what are you doing on the streets at this hour? A you a lost?"

"No. I am a stray."

"Ah. so you are the stray… what a cruel world it is… even a dog as cute as you are abandoned."

"Eh… I don't remember the last time a dog like you were left out… it is only the dogs who are ugly who are told to a leave."

"Ah… he must have been haughty. And you a deceived us."

"Deceived you? How?"

"Well, you a come here all bubbly and floating- we a mistook you for the type a dog who sits in a handbag. We a mistake you for being a, as those humans a say, 'a good boy,' a when you really a little rascal."

"Oh. he the type to be weary about brotha… he the type who gonna act a nice and kind to you, but then pull out a glock when you aint a lookin, ain't that so?"

"Ouh, we better be a watching out."

"What?" Questioned the lonely dog.

"A I a see… but what has got you in such a mood?"

"What are you saying? What mood am I in?"

"Ah you see… he is pulling a maneuver on us as we speak."

"Yeah… I a don't trust in this look of his… he is a classic case of covert criminal."

"No! No! What are you saying? I am just a simple dog. Why am I a criminal?"

"Ah… but then why are you in such a mood?"

"What mood am I in?"

"Please! you are either a tryna deceive us, or… explain… why are you on the streets?"

"Yeah… a pupparoo like a you… you don't belong on the streets unless you a bit poor missy's leg."

"No. I didn't bite anyone's leg. I don't understand…. Why are you so suspicious?"

"We ain't suspicious, we are just intrigued. For we a never see such a case. I mean… look at you… you are a practically dancing and… to be on the streets… how… well… if I were ever a house dog, I would be a lookin to go back to my a spoilt kingdom… for which fool a would a leave the good of a warm home to be on the streets and not a try to go back?"

"No... No. You have it all wrong. I was just abandoned. Why? I don't know. I am still trying to figure it out, but alas, I had tried searching for closure and I had seen my old maiden, yet she had simply fluttered her hand and thus I knew not to go to her and so, I am wondering the same thing as you. Maybe you say I am cute, but perhaps I am not cute enough."

"But, brother... can you imagine... he is a floating around the streets like a butterfly."

"Yeah... something is a off... how is it you are so jolly and joyous. Something is not adding up. Imma say, he has found some of that liquor in a dumpster."

"Yeah... and imma ask a you boy... where can we a find some of that?"

"No. No. Dear. Imma just tell you... I think I am in love."

"In love? You see a that brother... he is all silly willy... making up stuff... he is either on some of that white powder that the humans love or he is deceiving a us. A dog sayin he a in love... what type of nitty witty jokes he tryna pull."

"Calm my boy... I think a he may not be a lyin... I heard that house dogs sometimes a feel this way... they feel like a human... for a remember... there was that boy we met and he would always steal a leg a chicken from his kitchen and take it to that bitch up on main street. He also a claim to be in love..."

"Yeah, I woulda ate the piece myself… not even a share it with my dear ol brother here."

"Oh you a better share!"

"Ah… you see, we are the dogs of the street… we don't share outta love, but outta consequences and here he my brother but I would be the first one to steal a his lunch if I could."

"A wait a minute! Just'a minute. What a actually happened to that damn rabbit we caught earlier?"

"I a told you… honest my brother… it was the eagle… he swooped a down a snatched it."

"Even though we hid it in the bushes?"

"Yeah… you don hear the crows squawking the other day about them eagles having super vision or a something like that. They can see through walls or something a like that. Ah… but hold on a minute my dear friend… you see a what this fella a here do… he start a deceivin on us… he hadn't even spoken a much and we a was just suspicious of him and now he make a you suspicious of a me. Imma tell you a something… he tryna pull a maneuver on us, like we some kinda fools out on the street."

"Oh woof! I a see. He a deceptive little son of a human. There just isn't a something right about these strays- like a you ever hear of a dog in the streets a fallen in love."

"Well… hold on just a minute… I mean… maybe there is a explanation for it. Like I mean, we wild dogs out here simply tryna survive and so a… remember, that a boy down on

Sheppards Lane... the sheep dog we a met... he talking all psychological and stuff... explaining about how he a use mind control on the sheeps and stuff."

"Oh yeah. He was a funky fellow... with the big coat... at least he a farm dog, so he knows a the value of honest work, he a knoweth how to get a down and dirty... unlike this a young fellow here who be deceiving us, while a we a think he in love in the cold streets."

"Nah, a remember he was a explaining to us about that psychologist guy- a maslow or something like that... he was a sayin, we a first gotta a fill our bellies and then we can a get a feeling of companionship."

"But a look at us, we a here hungry yet a still we full amigos."

"But a you just said you was gonna eat the chicken without me."

"Aw. well you a take things a too seriously... I was only pulling your tail."

"And ah you a boy... so you a tell me you in love... so where are you getting your food from?"

"Oh. I am still hungry. But I do find food in the trash often."

"See he a back at it again with the deceivin. He a dangerous fellow. Telling us of the being in love and telling us that he on an empty stomach."

"Nah... well, this a time, I will have to disagree with you. Not on his deceptions... for I still don't trust him. But Ill a tell ya... I don't a trust a farm dog too, especially that dog tellin us a bout talking to the cows in their sleep. He a wild fella. Imagine… he a have a box… a coop I a think he call it, full of chickens and he a guardian it… he too is a deceiving us… none of these dogs a kept by humans can be trusted… a which dog gonna have a box a chickens and not take a bite… imma tell you… a dog you cant a trust."

"You see thats a it… these dogs, they all a strange when they kept by them human… and looka here… you ever see a dog in the wild look a like him? He a strange fella for a dog… he don't even look like he a growl."

"I can growl."

"Well a show us."

And at this the lonely dog tensed his jaws, but merely hissed.

"Ah you a see… he a don't know how to growl, so either he is a deceiving us again or he a right human… falling in love and all."

"Yeah I see a here. What type of joyous dog lives in this world who don't a need to growl… he a never even learn how."

"No wonder he a fallen in love… for love is something of the softhearted and he a never exposed to the life on them streets here. Oh for on tha streets, there is no a love for a doggo, we here… us wild dogs a never felt love in our life…

"not even our mothers loved us"

"And a so we don't even know what love is."

"And... and I know you a been loved before... I a see you dogs of the house, for all of us dogs of the streets have the eye of envy upon you dogs of the house. You might as well be a human."

"Infact, I a seen some dogs been a treated better than a human. I a once saw a human slap another human for bringing her a some roses and then I saw the same woman kiss her dog for a nothing at all... as if her dog is somehow deserving of that kiss... I a at least respect the man for his effort, but oh, how I a hate that dog... he was a fat boy... doing a nothing in his life a but a sleeping in a comfy bed, while we fools on the streets thin as a bone."

"Ah I a don't understand. Why did she a slap him?"

"Yeah, neither do I. A humans are a weird breed... I a mean, they a feel a love."

"And then they a hate the feelin too. I a still wonderin why did she a slap him? Was there something wrong?"

"Nah. he looked a honest a man... and imma say, us a street dogs... we a know a honest man and a scoundrel when we a see one... we are not a stupid human... we a have a sense you know and we can a smell where he a been. But that is humans for you... weird... a perhaps a she didn't like to be loved but a she a likes to give the love."

"Ah... humans... a strange creature indeed. And you... oh stray dog... it makes sense now... you a know what love is... so you a can be in love, for you were that boy who lived down by corktown... I a remember you now. You were that bratty girl's dog."

"Don't call her that!"

"A why not?"

"She is my mother."

"She is a your mother?... I a tell you she is a worse mother to you than a wild bitch. She abandoned you for nothing. Unless you are a deceiving us and you a bit her leg there, she had a just left you out in the cold for a nothing. And think... she took a you away from your actual mother... and she a one of the same people who have their wants and a needs. You know what them humans do these days... they a breed dogs to be a weak... so them dogs always be subservient to them... and a look at you my boy... what a body you have... and what face and a what... you don't a even know how to growl."

"A yeah... you are lucky you here are so damn adorable, or else I a tell you, we wouldda or another one of us from the pack, we wouldda already punctured you from the throat. You wouldda never survived out in the wild, for you were never bred to be for the wild, but bred to be a slave to the house- you were a raised to be a weak. A maybe our mother hadnt given us all love and daisies, but she a taught us to be tough and you a here wouldn't a last a day, if us pack didn't accept you."

"Yeah, you a remember what had a happened to the wolfs who a came from the north."

"Yeah we had a full war with em. You can see, half a my tail is a gone," and he flickered his tail and lo and beheld, half of it was missing. "You see… we had a full war… a many other dogs didn't make it out, but I assure a you. All them wolves are a gone. And we ate them for dinner like cannibals. But what can we a do… we are savages."

"And brother, I remember that a stupid dog who ran away from his house, kept complaining a so much about everything. He a said he was abused and a stuff and I thought well, now you on the street and you a better be quite, but he a never stop his yip yappin and a barking loud in the middle of the night and tryna be a tough, so I faced a him in a duel and I a slit his throat. Dumb dog didn't know how to be quiet. And he made a fine meal. But don't a worry boy, as long as you a don't be barkin in the middle of my nap and being so obnoxious as a him, we wont a hurt you. But him… he needed to go. Dumb dog."

A slither of fear now perturbed across The Lonely Dog, but now the other twin joined in, "a don't be worrying, you seem a fine fella. A little human, but nah, you don't seem to be of the annoying type. And a look, we may be from the streets, but we moral dogs, we dont kill for no reason. And even that puny squeaker, he was killed in a duel. You see we kill respectfully, we aint murderers. And a you can always reject a duel, but no respectful dog kills another dog without warning. Oh except the alpha- that is the one rule of power- if you the alpha, you can be killed in your sleep." As if that was suppose to ease his nerves about being eaten by a bunch of cannibal dogs.

"But anyway, a look, the sun is to rise... and we are to be off to find us some goldfish before the old man wakes up. See them human, so dumb, they a leave a pond full of fish in their front yard... as if us dogs don't have eyes. You can a join us if you want."

"Sure, I'll join. I am hungry and also I want to know something."

"Aight. Let's a talk whilst we a walk. I aint tryna have a run in with the gardener and he up early every mornin to water the plants."

"Yeah. How come you have to challenge every other dog to a duel, but not the alpha."

"Oh, and a remember neither in war, for sometimes another pack a think they can come through our land and start a hunting without our consent. In fact, a every once in a while they do come and we a deal with them as tourists and in that case the alpha always have a talk with them and see their intentions. For some of these dogs are no good and they a come in here tryna cause a trouble, shaking up all the wildlife, scaring even them flies and then our whole ecosystem is a disturbed. It's just they don't even care, for they don't live here, so they just a toss away their worries and behave however they like and we can't a have that. We gotta protect our land, ya know. And if you wish to kill a tourist you have gotta challenge them to a duel. And in fact, any dog you must a challenge to a duel, unless its an alpha or a war, like with them damn wolves. Except of course, if the alpha tells us to assassinate someone, like that one tourist who was disturbing the pups. He was tryna do the nasty with them two young ones and we weren't having none of that. Or then there was a that one fellow from our own pack, who tried and a kill without a duel and so we a took care of him in his sleep. "

"Yeah . You know, we two are a known out here as the assassin twins, for we take care of all them assassinations. And we get paid a pretty bone each for each job we do, for the alpha always has a thick stash... a sort of economic reserve to keep up the laws and orders of our society."

"Ahh... and yes... that's a why the alpha doesn't have to be challenged to a duel and you can kill him in cold blood. For it is that simple, if you don't like the way he a holding the city and you think you can do a better job, you have the right to assassinate him. It is a means to make a sure that the alpha is not the alpha simply because of his strength but a rather because he is a good ruler of the pack, else it would be a strong dog like that old big blackie who has the crown, yet he a real dumb one, my guy."

"Oh yeah. He is a so stupid, he a thinketh that he saw aliens one night, but a really it was us playing him for a fool. Aliens... a really? I mean, okay, if we a put effort into the prank, we coulda give him the pass, but a we did a nothing but shake one of them old garbage cans and rumble some of them cans and he a thought the aliens were telling him the secrets of the universe."

"Oh a man. And he a once told me he thought the owls were a conspiring against us."

"Nah. I believe that. You see them owls. I a tell you, they always upto no good."

"But brother, he said, they were rounding an army to take us to the caves and use us as slaves. How would a they do that? They eat mice. And ol blackie say that they can fly us up to the cave on the hill. And I wonder which one of these enchanting bitches told him that? I still a wonder to this a day, who coulda pull something like that outta their cheeks."

"Yeah he prolly mistook that shit for some of that dog food that them humans make which look clean like a feces."

"Oh. I say it may not look so good, but I a tell you brother, that a taste a hella fine. I tried some off the shepherd dog once and now I understand why he don't kill them chickens."

"Oh yeah. I remember, I was with you and I a must say, this here this stray dog with us, might a get sad if he remembers it, for nothing out here a taste so fine like it. They eatin for a pleasure, while we out here with our toes in the water catching fish in the cold."

"But I a tell you, fish always taste a better when you catch it yourself. Or anything taste better when it comes from honest effort my friend."

"Oh and a yeah... so... you can always kill the alpha, but a remember if you do, you will a have to be the alpha, until you a die and by that you will either die of old age if you rule good, or you shall be a killed if you don't. And lets a be honest, who wants to be the alpha? What a job that is!"

"Oh yeah... I mean, to be honest, our alpha, he is the laziest son of a bitch ever, but a no one wants his job, so a no one had killed him yet and I think he knows it, so he don't even sleep with one eye open. I mean that takes some balls, I must a say- he a really not doing much and in any other pack, he woulda been attacked many a times, but nah, for us dogs, we are too lazy and he knows it, so when he sleeps he doesn't even think to be weary. And fair to him... I am a just tryna enjoy life- I don't want to be the alpha. I just want some food, some sex and some of them booze we find in the trash every once in a while. I really am a simple dog."

"But brother, give him a break- he a getting old- he use to be quite the visionary when he was a younger- I mean, he did expand our land and take care of those rascal skunks and he is well experienced from his younger days and to be honest, he is prolly gonna die soon anyway and then, who shall be the alpha? Oh dear, we gonna have a real issue when that happens. now arn't we, for I a fear aint nobody want to a do that job."

"A hey, hey... a maybe you should do it." And he nudged the lonely dog, as they now began to enter the yards, as day was breaking behind the cloudy cover, now illuminating in that gray light the red maple leaves that were scattered across the yard. "Me?"

"Yeah... a why not? You would a relieve a lot of dogs out here, ya know? And its not like anyone shall care what you a do... unless... unless that is, some dogs suddenly becomes ambitious. One of them puppies that is playing as of now suddenly has a vision and decides he want to rule for he can do something he reckons great... for then... then, you must either do a better job than he could think himself capable or you gonna have to run away and a hide or you gonna die."

"Oh yeah... a you better run far and hide a tight, for remember we are the assassins. And a we don't wanna hurt you, but a we gonna have to follow the orders of the dog- and we cant let an alpha who abandons us live on, ya know? Its a nothing personal, but it's simply the way of the wild dog. And I hate to say it to ya, but we are really the best in the business. We a once had to cross two territories to assassinate one of them dogs who uffed a bad impression on our alpha and so we ran through each territory in full stealth mode and then finally when we got to his territory we had to fight a few of his buddies. But in the end, we a returned with his head and none other packs even knew of what was going on."

"But yeah, I remember the ruckus it all started, for then that the dog, whos head we brought back- his a pack started a war with the neighboring pack, for they thought that we were simply allowed to a go through their land- they a thought we had some sort a wrongful deal with them, but little do they a know we just the best… no one even knew that we had passed through a twice."

"And ya know how we a did it?"

"We found went to the wild grasses up north, the now barren land, for thats a where the wolves use to be and we a now own that land, but who in their right mind would want to live there- a barren joke of a place. But a yeah, we went up there and found a skunk and we a caught it and cover ourselves it its stench and thats a how we covered our scent."

"Anyway… enough chit chat… We don't have a long before that damn human comes out and ends our fun."

"And also remember, yeah, too much a splishin and splashin and the fish go dishin n dashing, so stay still and let the fish come to you- thats a when you a strike!" Remarked the other dog, as they finally entered the waters of the pond.

And so, with all said and done, The Lonely Dog seemed to have found friends... dangerous friends, yet at least they were friends nonetheless.

Enter the Gardener

Scene: the three dogs now sat under the old maple tree, each chewing at the fish between their paws, surrounded in the surreal air of the red leaves upon the yellow grass and chilly yet humid autumn air.

Gangsta 1:

(as he was breaking the spine of a fish between the canines that clasped the side of his snout):

KA-KA-KA-KA! (His jaws sawed into the bone).

Huh. I a tell you boys... I a tell you now. Listen to me straight! If this time that old punk of a gardener comes through imma show him... imma show him we aint playing no games... we hear on business... imma do him dirty like imma do this fish. He come here tryna tango and imma tango his leg right off, just like this: Pop!

(The fish bone finally snapped and with half a fish in his mouth he chewed it loosely as if he was an alligator).

And while Mr.Gangsta 1 was still chewing at his fish, as if by some twisted means... as if the writer of this script was tryna play a joke upon this tough doggy, in came the gardener.

96

The gardener:
(broom in hand)
Ahh! I a told you last time! U ain't gonna come back here! I tell
you.
(And the gardener now leaned up to them shaking his broom,
ready to strike and the three dogs got up immediately.
Gangsta 2: Oh brotha. Looks like you have the opportunity to
show us now, don't you!
Gangsta 1: screw that. He's got a stick and the vet don't come
cheap these days. Dash! Dash I tell ya. DASH!

And with that the three gangsta dogs dashed outta there,
chased by the gardener still waving the broom in his hands and
in his run, our menace, Dr.Danger himself, Mr. Gangsta 1
dropped his fish upon the grass and off they went, between the
fence and into the streets, where they further ran and ran, until
they reached the tail of the park.

Gangsta 2: Oh! How tough you are. You hero. You absolute hero!

Gangsta 1: My man. He a had there a cane and yall know it aint
a fair fight! How am I supposed to even pounce upon a thing
that can whack me from afar?

Gangsta 2: you hear this dawg here... this dawg who claims to be a my brother... he a makin excuses fatter than that old fish he dropped and now imma bet he about to ask for a sharing from our fishies.

Gangsta 1: oh no... no... no. You have it all a wrong. I was a full, so I left the fish behind on purpose. Like a message... u know. I remember seeing that a movie through a window once- what was it called? Yes. The Godfather. Yes. The man left a horses head in his bed- a sort of intimidation tactic and so I decided I'd a leave a fish head on the garden a sort of intimidation tactic... so he a know who he a messin with and a nobody messes with me and a gets away with it! Imma show him.

The lonely dog: yeah... sure.

Gangsta 1: yall dont a believe me?

Gangsta 2: not even a squirel is dumb enough to believe a what you be sayin. My boy, just take the loss and bite into some of mine.

The lonely dog: actually take the rest of mine. I'm actually full and my adrenaline is too high to eat anymore.

And so… gangsta 1 started chewing upon the leftover fish.

The lonely dog: wow. That was actually really fun. I enjoyed the chase. Like it was… exciting. I felt like I was a sort of criminal. Like perhaps Escobar running from the police.

Gangsta 1: ahh I see. So now u a gangsta. U understand that peculiar fun of crime. You understand the brotherly camaraderie. And perhaps now you a understand why little boys, rich as a rat in the trash, be a stealin candy from the local corner store.

The lonely dog: ah yes… Now I understand.

Gangsta 2: man I think it's important for these teens to be so illogical as to become thugs- for with such haughty naughtiness they a… a… understand the concept of youth! And oh. I remember eavesdropping on that old man who use to sit on that a there bench under the old oak.
(And he pointed to the other side of the park).
Yeh. He was a sayin to his grandson, that he a only had one regret of his teenage years, and that he didn't even regret it, for he knew it would've been a mistake, but he did feel like he wouldda wished to act more a fool when he was that age. Act more suspiciously… he wished he was in detention more and he

wished he had ended up in a penitentiary. But alas... he did remark that he was being ridiculous and that such a romantic life woulda been a cruel thing. But here the thing innit... I too understand that this life of ours... a complete scoundrelry, is one of tight friendship and excitement and joy and perhaps helps us realize something important... and I don't a know what that is... but hell... if I was rich I might still a be robbin candy from the corner store. And hell...

Gangsta 1: oh man... we a see your point... we see, you're a fanatic!

The lonely dog: No. I understand! I understand completely! For the first time in my life... I have experienced thrill. I see why so many kids are to be so seduced by the: as they say... the thug life.

Gangsta 2: oh yes! And I mean... perhaps its wrong... you know... us two fools have gotta rob, for we are anarchists and this is our protest against the soddy humans who have so splendidly leave food in the trash for us... and so because there is an excess of possibilities to legally obtain our food, we have become wretched... but alas... we atleast have morals, for we have covered our a unethical behavior under a fictitious label: we say we are revolutionaries and thus all of a sudden, we are no longer acting immorally when we a steal... ya see... the beauty of literature and ideology... hah!

Gangsta 1: hells yeah... we are gangstas because we are lookin for social change!

Gangsta 2:Change society how? Change it for the better? To both those questions I shall answer: we don't a know! But alas... now that you have a joined us... I have revealed to you the secrets of our stable consciousness and to tell you if any here fool tells you a to behave, u tell em to 'stop messing with the revolution, bloody, good for nothing goody-two-shoes."

Gangsta 1: and yeah. Give em a paw in the face while ya at it too.

Gangsta 2: nah a donr do that... we maybe gangstas but we a don't promote unnecessary violence my man... us gangstas are actually the most moral of all street dogs and hood rats... and now u too are a gangsta, so u gonna be riding it out with us... we brothas now... u rely on us and we rely on you... ya know.

And for the first time in a long time, The Lonely Dog was no longer lonely and thus he became: The Gangsta Dog.

The Rapper Dog

"Check me... a check me... lemme spit some for you." As they
now sat back at the underpass and his brother started
beatboxing.
"I just a left the garden after feedin
So now im a be spittin.
Then later I be a cockin
My glock in
The back and come through- no stoppin...
Me...
Cuz ur brain I be a poppin
And I get ur girl to do the moppin."

Now they switched between their roles.
"With my ak I be lickin
The the house of a chicken
And then check in
And I see he a dog that checked out
I call that a hot dog
And I got a hot sock
On my hot glock...
I a mean I stay silent on the block."

And then they both looked at the lonely dog and began:

"And now its a your turn."

"Wait... what?"

"Yeah. You a gotta spit some bars for us."

"What... no... I don't know how."

"What you mean u dont know how?"

"Don't think too much. Just do it! Like u wearing a quad a Nikes on your paws boy."

"Yeah. Dont think fool. Just spit boy! Just spit! Ya feel me."

"Just spit!" Replied the other and at that exact moment they both began mixing a beat, indicate that they wouldn't except any refutations and so thus did the lonely dog become the rapper dog:

Ahhh...

...Explosive....

 Like gas in the socket....

Or a glock in ma pocket.

...

...And like a poggo I bop it.

Heart stoppin.

With square pants, I'll bob it.

And I see she a sob, innit.

Cuz I so flawless

Even tho im lawless.

Imma be bossin,

so don't be floppin,

or my wings imma flapit.

And with my gat imma get it.

A draco look real hip, but an ak gonna make u hop.

When I gonna get the gun out.

 Gonna spit and u gonna splatter... ur head served on a platter,

no cap cuz im a rapper not a capper.

 Yabadabadoo.

Feel like scooby doo

cuz i solved the mystery: who done it?

 Me. I did the deed.

 The body buried in the reeds,

 Besides this bazooka smokin like a hookah. And even the cops

got spooked, yeah.

"Ouuhh damn boy!"

"And he a say he cant rap. He a say he cant. U hear this fool?"

"I a tell u he tryma deceive us. But man cant anymore. U see he

a real rapper. He a real gangsta. He a learnin fast. And a damn, brotha u a better watch out cuz he is the real problem on the street!"

"Oh damn. Yeah yeah... this boy is a killa and..."

And the rapper dog now began to glance around as one does when humbled by the awkwardness of receiving compliments and then as he was turning back to look at the gangsta dogs, he thought he saw something and he quivered for a second as his eyes dilated.

And so he turned back to make sure he didn't imagine it.

But no he didn't!

It was her. It was her! And he saw her and now looked at her, as she watched him from behind the branches of a bush and then they looked at each other for a moment... long was the moment... short was the moment... for time as we have already expressed is a weird concept and when a boy is in love, he sees time even more perplexing of an apparition and so he stared at her and she stared at him and they made that feint eye contact which occurs at distances and then she smiled, winked with what seemed like a bit of embarrassment and then dashed again behind the bushes.

As he saw her leave he seemed to smile in blush and yelped, "It's her. It was her! I just saw her." And the dogs who were still enchanted in their praise of The Rapper Dog, stopped in confusion and asked:

"Who?"

"What?"

And he grew slightly embarrassed as he replied, "the bitch I love."

"Oh. Where?"

"She just fled behind the bushes... I think she was watching me... oh... how embarrassing!"

"Embarrassed? Embarrassed!"

"Damn. Why the hell would you a be embarrassed... you were a killin it just now."

"Ya. Brotha, what is wrong with this fella? Why would he be embarrassed? It's not as if he completely botched it... in fact he completely butchered it and he a sayin he embarasses. My boy! What is wrong with you?"

And with that The Rapper Dog was reassured, both by relieving his insecurities and also by reminding him of his love, for he had managed to stop thinking of her that morning and now once again had the oxygen blown upon the fire in his heart, resurging the passions of his desire.

Watching the birds

The white bitch sat there in the grass on the ends of the field, near the forest and upon entering the valley between the bushes, he saw her and they locked eyes and since he was near enough, he took a few more steps along the edge- the edge that separated the bright, sweet valley from the shaded canopy... the split between chaos and order? Let's work on the description later.

"Hi."

"Hi," She wooed back in that sweetly innocent manner that young and dreamy puppies make- yet it wasn't in that overbearingly annoying manner of childhood, but rather in that manner of youthful manner of elegance that befalls upon a natural- for she was a natural- a being of sweetness, like a sort of earthly incarnation of that archetypical force of feminine growth that people have personified as 'Mother Nature'. And in such natural guile, one is calmed, yet excited. One is perplexed yet enchanted in the thrills of simplicity. For it was so human... so natural being this interaction, for she smiled in that happy manner to forfeit any thoughts of a one-sided approach to the matter of the heart that is the drear of any human trying to achieve that goal of courtship.

And so with ease, the dogs were both comfortable, yet still in obvious excitement, which when sensed, increases the excitement into an jittering anxiety, yet that same sense of excitement also induces a greater calm and so here lieth that dual increase of opposites, which form the equilibrium of the heart- an equilibrium which is of the stabilization of the mind and body upon that highly heightened plane of energy- the surging thrust of oxytocin, serotonin and like upon cool water one goes toes in, yet plunges through- that shock of cool energy now jolted through the bodies of them both. That is how to describe it- when one takes a polar plunge- or an iced shower- that state perfectly symbolizes this state of which the dogs now were in. Cool, yet bursting in shivers with energy- heightened energy- for this love was energetic like cocaine, yet calmly euphoric like opium. Yes, and so in this state they could continue, not an awkward conversation, but a loving conversation, where passion was kindled on both sides. The type of conversation, where awkwardness makes it better for both- for both can laugh- for both are interested- and so for both, each represents that impossible perfection that they both know well, dear and certain doesn't exist in one another- yet, still each flaw is accepted as a virtue: now that is that maturely childish perfection that had existed, yet obviously unacknowledged to the dogs, for who can acknowledge such a thing in such a moment, in such a state when their mind were set arace in this two-sided display of affection. Now no matter how true, or how false the reality of all this was, if our lonely dog had a diary, here he would write: "oh she loves me and I love her. I am in love. We are in love. What a beautiful moment it was. Or perhaps an eternity."

And despite the uncertainty of the truth, all that matters is what the lonely dog perceived, for thus, that is life... an experience of self-centered perceptions. And as this dog had now began the breaking of his perception of time and reality- an indication that points to the truth being that he was in love- for words aren't enough to truly understand the heart, yet a person's perception of the world tell us everything- so thus, now the lonely dog became: The Love Dog. And one might think, is this not too much perception for such little contact- but one must remember this is a fairytale, that should, but no longer exists in society past a certain age- that age being the age when the pessimism of realism becomes a mentality that is adopted by the mass man or woman. And it's unfortunate, that we grow up- and that is to grow out of nature, for do beings not become like children when in love? And thus, from such a question, we must reconstruct our next question: do children not love more than adults? And so, indeed- this fairytale is true for children and animals- for... us adults are broken... for us adults no longer are able to love quickly, yet we are lucky to grow for our capacity to love is replaced with another skill, for instead of being able to love quickly, the adult is able to produce prejudice more quickly- the most important of all traits in modern society- for what else is possibly so unnatural as prejudice based upon insignificance? And what else is the goal of society other than to take us away from nature? Ah, we may not love, for modern society holds the only love: the love of vanity. And what a love it is!

"What are you doing?"

"I am sitting. Watching the birds and the children." She said with that hint of nervousness, as she started playing with her paws, as often people do to ease their body in such excited states of fantasy.

"Yeah... you see anything interesting today?"

"Ah. You see, I saw a bluejay today... I haven't seen one in a while. And look there." She then pointed her snout into the trees to her left and they both looked up, providing that brief moment of relief from the intensity of eye contact, "there are two cardinals there. I love the cardinals. They are so beautiful and exotic. And they often dance. I always feel as if I am in a foreign land when I see them. Just look at them." They both watched them for a moment and then she began again, "Do you ever watch the birds."

"Not really. I once met an owl, but he wasn't too friendly, so I didn't really befriend him. And this one time, I fought with a woodpecker. I still remember it. He just wouldn't stop making all that noise. You believe it. He was pecking upon the metal slides in the park and I was trying to take a nap. Why would he possibly be doing that? There are obviously no worms there. I bet you, he was just trying to wake us dogs up. So I told him to stop and he said, 'sorry, I'll stop right away and then I returned to under the oak where I was napping and as soon as I lied down, he started again. So I went up to him and I asked him... why are you doing that? And you'll never believe what he told me."

"What?"

"He said he was looking for worms in the metal."

"Maybe he was drunk."

"Oh no! The way he was moving his head, he definitely wasn't drunk. Maybe he did something else- but drunk... no. And so, I told him, there are no worms in the metal and then, guess what he said."

"What?"

"He said, 'no shit Sherlock,' and so I had it with him. And so I climbed the slide and then he even tried to peck at me, so then I pecked him with my paw and away he fell to the floor. I mean, I didn't hurt him. I hope. But he was really ripe to get a beating- at least it was from me, not from the owl, for he wouldda prolly ate him for breakfast. But yeah- a woodpecker pecking on metal. It sounded as if we were in the middle of a battlefield. I even saw some kids running, as if Freddy Krueger had just entered the park with a machine gun."

"Wow. I never knew woodpeckers were such a menace."

"I mean, I never had an issue with woodpeckers before, but this one... he was just something else. Anyway... what's your favorite type of bird?"

"The woodpecker." And they both giggled a little, as soon as The Love Dog had realized it was a joke by her playful smile. "Nah, actually I don't have a favorite- all of them are beautiful and all of them make each other more beautiful- my favorite thing is how nature completes itself- how one species is completed by the existence of another species."

"And what do you think about humans?"

"Oh. Humans. Humans are an interesting animal. I can never understand them! They are just so... so... complicated. I mean... they are so stupid... they make all sorts of complications out of the world for no reason, which makes their lives more complicated and confused and... ah... just painful for them and then through all those stupid complications they make a solution to the problems they made. Like they are so... perhaps... bored. I mean, to sum up all of human behavior, I see them as being so bored that they make problems for themselves so they can find the solution and then say to themselves that they are very smart- yet... okay... you found a solution: congratulations! But wouldn't it be smarter to have never caused the problem in the first place. So complicated- so stupid. I have never seen an animal that thinks they are the smartest animal, except human beings- for they are so stupid that they think they are smart. Oh. And yeah... I love humans, for they are the most interesting animals to watch."

"Ha... you know what that reminds me of. I remember once watching this movie, and a father was talking to his son. And his father said, 'boy, hang around smart people, for then you will become smart like them.' And the son said, 'dad I hang around stupid people, because they are the ones who truly make you smart.' And the father asked, 'why is that son?'"

And then unexpectedly, the white bitch continued it: "And the boy replied, 'Because you can learn what to do to be smart from reading books, but what you can't learn is how to be stupid, except by observing stupid people. So, I hang around stupid people to learn all the things I shouldn't do if I want to be smart.'" Haha. They both laughed and then she continued, "Sorry, I couldn't help it- I loved that movie! What was it called?"

"I have no idea- I just remember watching it once."

"Yeah... it was hilarious. Do you watch movies often?"

"I used to. Not much anymore though. What about you?"

"I go down to the docks every Saturday, as the fishermen usually are watching a movie in their shack, so I go there and sit on the pier and watch through the window. You should come next time."

"Alright- it's a date." The Love Dog replied, only realizing what he said after the words left his shocked snout.

"Okay," she giggled, "we'll be just like the humans and go on a movie date."

Moby Dick

Upon the sandy path upon the beach, walked the two dogs- the love dog and his beloved white bitch- as the evening was now arriving. Through the slightly overcast sky, the raging rays of the evening sun bellowed in its glory and the two sat upon the white shores to watch it settle below the autumn tides and in so, the fall wind harassed their eyes, as the southerly winds of the sea whistled in announcement of its foolish entry into town. And thus happened the dip of light and the times were changing. The sky was changing. The lights were changing. The moods were changing. The dogs... the dogs were changing. The nightly energy now enlivened the souls of the dogs and there still lie the fainting quivers of light from beyond the horizon, when the street lights began to glow. And as they looked out upon the views, paw in paw, The Love Dog- the cheeky fiend of romance looked upon the white bitch in all her grace and elegance, teary eyed by the teasing winds and stared at her. Aware of this, she still gazed upon the sea for another moment more and then returned the glance and it made the love dog laugh in that childlike giggle of love and so too the white bitch returned a sheepish smile and looked down in that exudinging awkward aura.

"The sunset was pretty, but you are prettier."

And his words made her blush. Flattered, she looked again upon him and lightly licked the side of his snout and then began to dig her head into his neck saying, "the sailors usually start watching their movie at sunset," and with that they began their ascent up the beach to the docks.

As they entered the harborfront, there was some commotion by the shack where the sailors were lounging.

"Aye! Aye! Lets drain the barrel of cider!"

And they all cried:"AYE!"

"And I tell you fellow comrades of the sea. Put on a movie!"

And they all cried: "AYE!"

"And I'll tell you! Say Ahoy to here dinner. For feast your eyes upon the fattest here cod you've a seen in years." And the seaman opened up a large bucket and pulled out a cod that was almost as fat as him and all the sailors cried: "Ahoy!"

"And set the coals a burning, for here we feast upon this ballooned fish that had a me confused in the waters, for he pulled like a whale."

And they all cried: "Aye! Aye! Set the coals. Set the coals!"

"And here, here... he is colossal like the white whale! He is a real Moby Dick! And I a say to that! Lets a watch Moby Dick tonight!"

And they all cried: Aye! Aye! Lets a watch a Moby Dick!"

And with that, a skipper turned on the tv and used a playstation controller to begin his search for the whitewhale upon the tv screen, while another one of them began pulling about the bag of coals and another cleaning the grill and another fumbled with the bag of spices.

"Moby Dick again?" Cried the white bitch.
"Aye!" Responded The Love Dog.
"This is the fourth time they're watching it this month. I mean it's a great movie, but dont they get bored?"
"Nay!" Responded The Love Dog smiling and then his smile grew cheekier, "I have a better idea than... instead of watching Moby Dick...lets... well you'll see. Just be prepared to run."
"Wait... what?"
"Oh you'll see. Trust me... it'll be better than watching Moby Dick tor the fourth time."
"Ah okay... but what are you planning?"
Just give me a minute." And with that The Love Dog slowly crept up to the shack and awaited the perfect moment.... And he waited... and waited... and then finally, the moment had come, for the fat sailor began to light his cigarette, while all the rest were busy in their preparation and with that he leaped. He leaped quick, yet quietly towards the bucket and grabbed the fish. As he did this, the weight of the fish brought the buckets tumbling down into a clanking and the fat sailor immediately

turned around with a half lit cigarette in his mouth and away they ran.

"Stop! Stop, I tell ye! That's theft! That's theft ye damn dogs! Ye damn crooks," he shrieked as his fat legs began to accelerate him like one of those huge 16-wheeler trucks- full of power, yet due to the sheer weight- not powerful enough. And he now chased the two dogs, dropping his tobacco stick to the ground, where it steamed upon the wet wood. And the two dogs ran out, while the fat sailor tried to catch them, but alas within seconds they had beaten him to the gate of the docks and were out into the street. And as they made their great escape into the night, they could hear him yell, "Damn Dogs! Stealing my fish!" But let us be honest, he never really had any chance of catching them and so he retired back to the shack. "Oh the bloody rascals. Oh the damn rascals. Oh... what fish that was... a marvelous fish... fatty and juicy... but alas... those damn dogs... if i a er see em again... if we a see them damn dogs again, we a gonna strangle em and eat em for dinner," he now a yelled to the shack. And they all replied: "AYE!" As another sailor pulled out an identical fish from the bucket and put it upon the grill.

The Blue Baboon II

Once again upon that perching balcony sat the two philosophers.

"You know... i'll tell you something."

"What's that?"

"I've come to this conclusion about life. A rather profound conclusion. Say, I'll tell you a proverb that explains all of the human condition."

"Lemme guess... I saw a fox catch a rabbit the other day and I felt sad for the rabbit but then I realized... ah life!"

"Nah. Actually I'll one up that this time."

"Alright! Now I'm excited."

"Well: life is like a monkey with a machine gun. You either have a good laugh or you get shot."

"Oh indeed. I like that one."

"Haha. Life is funny. I was sitting in the tub yesterday and I thought perhaps the most profound of things: the tub is the perfect metaphor for life. The water is either too hot or too cold and only for a brief minute of bliss is it ever perfect."

"Well I'll be damned- is that not the perfect metaphor for life?"

"And to add to that, when the water is right, are you not too agitated by the previous heat to appreciate it?"

"Oh well damn. I know I better remember that, for I know I too often forget to appreciate those moments of bliss."

You and me both… you and me both."

"Well doesn't everyone? I think they need to teach your philosophies in school."

"Oh well damn. Imma tell u something more."

"Please do."

"You see, all this talk makes me think of memories. And you see, it is always dangerous to think of memories by yourself. Do good memories not hurt as much as bad memories… just in different ways. But thus, we must always reminisce with others for then you have someone to share the pain with and the sharing of pain is called: laughter."

"Oh… well you'll have to give me a minute to understand that one. I hear you… lemme just think." And so they stared upon the starry night sky and sipped their coffee. "Now I'll tell you something. For I realize what you are saying and I must say I agree. And I will say… beauty… beauty is… well… true beauty… makes a man want to cry and so… through all this thought I have this realization. The realization of perhaps… the mechanism of beauty… What makes it so powerful."

"Lemme guess… knowing our droll minds, it's gonna have to do with pain."

"Well does pain not arouse our more extreme moods?"

"Oh indeed. And I must admit I am a big fan of bdsm."

"Why am i not surprised?"

"Oh... cuz u know I don't like vanilla."

"Ha. But vanilla has a place, does it not?"

"Indeed it does. But vanilla is not the topic of discussion. Get on with it! Who's keeping who in suspense now?"

"Well you see... It is the paradox between pleasure and suffering that is known as beauty. All beauty is a fantasy, which is pleasure, yet it is trying to comprehend the impossibility of this fantasy into reality that is suffering. Thus beauty is pleasure and suffering."

"Ah. Mate... I don't get it, explain."

"Ah... you see. Look upon beauty. Like the mountains, or the stars and tell me... does it not make you feel a fantasy? Beauty so immense... its hard to believe- for all true beauty is something so perplexing that it's hard to believe."

"Oh. The lesbian... I have never see something so cute... I feel... I feel... oh. Her eyes... deep brown and large and her cheeks... ah! And yes! I can't comprehend her beauty... when i see her... I feel... I feel... I want to do something, but I don't know what? And I know, no matter what I do is never enough to comprehend her beauty. I can never possibly fully comprehend this fantasy that she is into reality... she seems like something from a different reality and so thus... she is suffering! And so...

even if I had her... I would suffer... for she is simply too damn beautiful! And so... is not all romance suffering... oh I see! All beauty involves suffering. And yes... I do feel that pang in my heart when I see the mountains and then find that I cannot understand what I am looking at... for that is beauty. But alas... the lesbian! The vision of her. The movie in my mind.... Oh you have ruined me, friend! For I am now suffering from the image of beauty... for you have now made me have a good memory! And here we are not laughing... so quick! Tell me a joke... so that we may share the suffering! Ah! You are indeed an evil genius... you... you... have ruined my night with beauty."
"Here is a joke: life is like a monkey with a machine gun... you either get shot or laugh at your friend who has gotten shot until you get shot... alas... it's best if you both laugh while you cry."
"Damn you... you are indeed an evil genius!" And they both shared their suffering.

"But look... look... that's the dog I was telling you about." And they both looked as two dogs were running out of the dock side by side, one laughing, while the other smiling with a large fish wedged between his jaws.
"Oh looks, like they saw the monkey and they chose to laugh."
"Haha. Perhaps we ought to do the same now." And they continued to watch as the dogs made their great escape and an angry sailor burst through from around the shacks on harbor

front. "Damn Dogs! Stealing my fish!" And he threw his hat upon the floor and strode back into the docks with that gloomy anger that sailors are known for.

"Oh well... looks like he's the one who got shot."

"Oh... wise monkey of life." And they both laughed, for they knew that at this moment they weren't shot and thus the water in the the tub was of the perfect temperature and so, it was time to share the pain and appreciate the beauty of that blissful moment of perfection that so rarely knocks upon the door of experience and then he whispered, "I'll remember this night."

Dinner in the Lights

As the two dogs ran past the corner of the Blue Baboon, they now stopped on the adjacent street, where the bright strobe lights shone a mellow blue mood light, with highlights of a controversial bright pink and while all this happened, a smokey warm light radiated from inside, mixed with a hot yellow from a sign above the entrance that posted the cafe's slogan- a philosophical warning to all that stated: 'Eat Monkey Brains for Breakfast, Expect Banana for Lunch'. And under the slogan ran the name: The Blue Baboon. Ironically the word blue was illuminated in red, while 'the' and 'baboon' were lit in a calm smokey blue. The letters of the slogan were bubbly, the letters of the name were straight and chic, while finally under the last n in baboon began the word cafe in cursive and in red where the curvy tip of the capital C in Cafe overshot into the n and C's top trailing edge wrapped around the middle of the the right foot of this n character like a vine of ivy, in a manner that was subtle yet depicted the intermingling of opposites, yet the lights remained as a distinct red and blue rather than an exchange into purple- this seemed to express the philosophy of philosophy and so was much appreciated by any aestheticist.

 And through all the commotion of the calm air that enshrouded the two in the dance of the contradictory energies that bespoke the cafe via the cascade of brilliantly brocading

lights, they looked into each others eyes once again for a moment of time- that same moment that seemed to exist outside of time itself. That moment that seemed like the first moment and yet also the last... for at that moment everything seemed to disappear. Dissipate. For at that moment nothing else seemed to exist except the two dogs in the dusky twilight of the deep night. And in such a moment- and so perhaps because it was too intense, or for she was shy or for whatever reason, she began to speak, not once breaking that undrownable smile that had lit as soon as the dogs had begun their run. And indeed she tried to settle it down to speak, but as she spoke, she quivered, half in laugh, half in nervousness and half in excitement. "That was fun. I have never done that before." And with that she could feel her heartbeat becoming more and more pronounced and so too did The Love Dog's heart. Entangled in this mood, they both breathed steadily, yet mechanically and then she continued, "wow. You're so cool." And so, she had spoken something in fritter of that awkward emotion, that she immediately regretted, but The Love Dog smiled and kissed her cheek and she once again smiled excessively and her lips began to quiver as she tried to conceal it- yet all her cards had been seen and The Love Dog being a simple dog loved the sight.
And so now he continued, "where shall we eat?"
"Here is romantic." And with that they both ate in the dim lights of the street until there was nothing left but the slimy

stain of the fish upon the cool concrete and a few scales that scattered the light of the world upon their eyes, which seduced their dilated pupils deeper into the mysterious air of romance and they slowly began to dance together to that slow classical tune that echoed from within the walls of the cafe. And while the music ran through their bodies, they made their way through the streets yawning until they finally cuddled up behind a bush. She wrapped tightly within his underbelly and they kept warm, while staring up into the starry night, where the beginnings of clouds were now sailing in from sea. And so... they entered a sleep, yet did they dream? For who could differentiate reality from dream in such a moment of emotion? And they slept. And they slept till day break, where the love dog now awakened, finding the white bitch now even closer wrapped within him, clutching for all his warmth. And then he looked up and there it was: the first snow of the season, slowly gliding down toward earth from the heavens like fine sugar, flirting in the wind, where finally a thin, white, fragile flake glistened through the leaves in the bush and landed upon his black nose.

Ghosts exist

And as The Love Dog was a simple being, they enjoyed the simple gaieties of life like midday strolls in the park, hunting the white winter hare and playing all sorts of dog games. And one day upon their stroll, the white bitch noticed that upon seeing a couple walking together, The Love Dog grew a little anxious.

"What's wrong?"

"Oh. nothing."

"Tell me."

"Well. I have a secret: I'm a stray."

"Well that's no secret. Everyone can tell. No wonder you're so cute and cheery." And it made The Lonely Dog smile.

And then he continued, "you see that girl. She used to be my owner."

"Are you going to say hi?"

"Nah... she doesn't seem to acknowledge my existence."

"Oh... I'm sorry. I can't say I can imagine how it feels, but I do imagine that it doesn't feel good."

"Yeah. It kind of... hurts."

"But forget about her. You will always have me," and then she licked the side of his face and they both smiled.

Spring Love

And as expressed before, the two dogs enjoyed the simple gaieties of life through the calm of winter and now arrived the blooms of spring. And one fine morning, when the snow had all but just melted, The Love Dog was hit by a mellow breeze and he exclaimed: "rosebud!" And then took a heavy inhale as he left his den to find the scents of wild rose bursting through the air with its exotic sweetness. Rich and delightful. Elegant and pink... the smell was pink. The taste was white. For it was a pure smell that flowed around in a sort of thickness, that dampened the air with calm, yet too, excited and stimulated the senses. And the air was still frosty, which only added to the sweetness, especially since the atmosphere was still stale that morning, where a fog now rose steadily from the grounds, as the morning sun warmed the surface of this mighty, yet small planet that us grandly puny creatures inhabit. Oh... what a perspective... for what simple creatures one must become to have the intelligence to comprehend the vastness in the little- for is there not infinite complexity in simplicity; is there not simplicity in all complexity. And with such a perspective, how can a simple, stupid dog not possibly be a romantic? How can simple stupid not see the entire universe in one of those tiny dewdrops that now lay upon a rose thorn, that led up to the sweet bud, that was slowly on its way to rupturing into that magnificent flower: that mighty rose!

And so, we see, with such intelligence as this dog possessed he was simply a simple romantic and so he smiled tasting the rosehoney upon his gasp, "ah! Where is she?" And with her memory, an energy roared upon him- that energy which is desire. That desire to have her. That craving. That emotion. Perhaps it is this wantonness that makes everyone with significant intelligence act stupidly, for with such intelligence, one can appreciate the perplexity of truth- the truth of what matters and in so sepearting real desires from that of vanity, a being no longer veils themselves in a facade mended by the overly complex throughts of insignificant apparitions. Oh and so too, let us appreciate the unfortunate catastrophe that reigns supreme in contemporary society: what is truth is often masqueraded by what is in fashion.

And so, with all this humming of intelligent stupidity that flowed through The Romantic Dog, he began his search for his love. He began his search for that creature that symbolized harmony and perfection in nature. He began searching for the being that was the physical manifestation of his feminine half. He began searching for the girl that completed his existence- the girl that balanced his energies as a complimentary soul that fit into all his activities. He began to search for- dare I say: his other half. And so He began searching for the white bitch.

For the first time in his life, he felt like a dog.

He had looked everywhere that day, in search of his love and as evening came he grew a little anxious, "where could she be? Where did she go? It had actually seemed as if she had grown a little distant the past week and was completely absent the past few days and had started spending less time with him. But today was so nice a day, such a sweet romantic day and The Romantic Dog had searched everywhere for her and now finally decides to search the forest.
And so in the evening wind, as the sun began to set behind the ridges of the mountains, the romantic dog entered the enchanted forest, barking a woofing for her, yet finally as night struck, he was unsuccessful in his finding and thus he made his way back through the woods feeling that his efforts had been dejected hoping that she was well and safe.

As he now neared the park at the edge of the forest, he could hear some noise... a little rustling and muted voices which had caught his attention.
 And as he approached, step.. by... step... each foot placed upon the soft earth another step seemed to be placed within his

stomach, softening his gut. "Huh...huh...Huh..." a warmth... a dizziness... beginning between his ribs and running into his genitals... then his legs...then his head... and the warm dizziness numbed his whole body, as he continued to step further and further and further and further the symphony of panthing began to grow. And this dog now had a thought... but no! Impossible! But still he advanced for he heard it... he felt it... what was it? Something.... something wrong... and now swirling in that vertigo, he passed into a new consciousness, nauseated by fear as he could hear them more and more clearly and he heard her... her moan... her panting... and No! It couldn't be! And so he awakened in alertness... and then he reached the edge of the forest and... he saw.

He saw... He saw. It was her! And his jaw drooped, unable to comprehend what he was witnessing- experiencing. And all the numbness began to clench up back into his heart; all his anxiety began to recede into his eyes where it bubbled into tears and ruptured through into the world where it began to run across his shivering snout. Shivering for, the vertigo now took over his body in rapid convulsions of horror and he began to cry. Yet frozen, he still couldn't comprehend whether this was reality and the shivers now began to tremor through his body, where all the anxiety, numbness, rage, desire, despair, misery and mystery reacted and combusted into a violent pressure that now burst out of the chambers of his heart- cracking, splitting, shattering- and the shards flung themselves through his chest cutting at his lungs. "Huhhh...huhhh....huhhhh..."and the noise ran through him... what was it? What was this sound? Was it from that bitch as she was mating with betrayal? Or was it from his collapsed lungs? It was from her! From her! The bitch! For how could he sound when he couldn't breathe, except for a deep wheezing that echoed through him to his ankles that now collapsed, as his chest tightened to such a point that it seemed all his muscles moved in to choke him out. And now upon the floor he started spasming... spas...ming... twitching and a burning began itching within him for now Pandora's box had been opened and the anxiety flooded him. Ahhhhhhhh! He cried, but not a sound could come out of his constricted throat. And the sound... the sound... it haunted... it penetrated... it hurt.... ahhh... the pain now blistered his insides and he knew he had to leave ... he had to get out of there... he had to run- run away: Far Away!

And so.... He got up quickly and ran.... and ran ...and ran and ran. He ran as far as he could, but it wasn't far for while running, his vision began to blur- his head became light- his legs seemed to have nerve damage and upon the ground he fell and continued his twitching trying to grasp for breathe in struggling gulps that he only managed to take while fighting his immune system- for he felt like- like- like: Dying! Ahh! Life is a sickness and death is the cure! Ahhhh! Since the moment

he was born this little fellow had been kidnapped from his
mother, then had been abandoned to a shelter, then abandoned
by Lassie, abandoned by the children- abandoned by all humans
and now abandoned by: The Bitch! Ahhh! His life flashed before
his eyes and "AHHH! HOW PATHETIC I AM!" And then he
coughed violently, causing him to contort upon the floor, as his
face turned blue and... and he began to cry.

Black.

When he awoke... he immediately started to jitter... perhaps he
was jittering in his sleep. It was a quick nap- no- it wasn't a
nap- it was simply a loss of consciousness, for it seemed as if his
mind gave up- it simply couldn't take it anymore and so now he
awoke once again paralyzed in that state of uncontrollable
jitters and he could feel a raging heat running through his
body, but still he felt cold! And then all of a sudden, he began to
cry violently again and started to run again in that
lightheadedness that ran through his entire body and due to
this absolute vertigo he kept tripping, yet this time he got up
again... and he would trip again and yet get up again and again
and... again... until he finally reached the top of the mountain
in the north where he knew he would be alone, for it was where
no dogs lived, yet was still part of their territory. And here he
now looked out from the edge of the cliff and looked down

where he imagine they were probably still at it in the park below and then he looked at the moon in the clear sky and began to cry, looking out upon the few clouds that lined the distances. He then looked down. "Oh... shall I jump?" And with that thought, for he was too lazy to jump, he let himself fall...

While he glided through the air, once again time seemed to slow down and for a brief second he seemed to deny the pain any existence, for his mind had gone stale in expectation of the end...

And when he fell, he could feel the air running through his fur and the tears upon his face being lifted off by the winds of his fall....

And as he fell, he expected the end...

And as he fell he felt that his body had already died....

And as he fell... his mind disappeared into nothingness...

And as he fell he felt he was already dead...

And as he fell... the moonlight lit up his cute white and brown body, while the air lifted his ears and his tongue causing them to flutter in the wind as fluids stringed off his face- from his eyes, nose, snout and mouth.

And as he fell the moonlight caught these liquid strings and transformed them into shimmers of silky crystal webs that blazed upon the background of the cliff backdrops...

And as he fell...
He hit the ground.
The end.

Escapism

Upon awakening, the next morning, the lonely dog lie in a bush where a large branch lay under his sore, bruised back. It felt as if his backbone had shattered, yet... there was still this odd pump of adrenaline that flushed his muscles with a sort of energy. His eyes burned and his nose was dry, but soon all of him exploded once again as once again the jitter began! And once again the tears, the drool and the snot was pumped out of him through each violent quiver that sent his body into contortions and so... as he didnt know what to do, he got up and began to run again and once again he ran and ran and ran up to the top again, however this time, although numb, dizzy and prickly was he, his mind was empty- that violent memory seemed unable to register for his mind did not work anymore and so this time as he got to the top of the mountain he didn't cry anymore, although tears did still trinkle between his lids and stream down to mix upon his snout with his snot, but... but... he didn't...no... he couldn't register the reality of anything anymore and it would have been so perhaps due to the fact that he had to slow down to allow his mind to function- but this exact thing is what kept him from stopping and so he kept running and running... perhaps he was purposefully trying to stop himself from thinking, thus he didn't stop his legs or perhaps he... perhaps... perhaps he just didn't stop and perhaps he just didn't think and perhaps the two concepts of running and thinking have nothing to do with each other here... or perhaps .. perhaps... perhaps- and then that's when his legs collapsed... in the middle of his analysis of his theory of running and thinking did he fall upon the ground sliding through the grass as his legs seemed to run out of ability. And then alas... he lied there in shock... this time still... still not thinking of anything and still... his body was still and it was at this moment that he realized he was dead...

And here lie the lonely dog upon the grass believing he was dead due to the shock he was still trying to process and so... he lay there, paralyzed for days, still believing he was dead until he finally fell asleep and entered upon death.

The end.

A realization of life

Once again. He woke just like he did yesterday and the day before that and the day before that, however this time there was something different: he realized he wasn't dead.

Stillborn

The next day once again he awoke. But he still lay there.

Genderal Dualism

Finally two more days had gone by and now on the third he awoke. Yet this time he moved. He got up. Walked a bit and then collapsed again. And then he lay upon the ground for a while and all of a sudden he began running again. However this time, there was something different... something had changed in him and so came evening when he stopped running and now stood back on the edge of the cliff where now a tempest of emotions engulfed this young lonely dog.

Intoxicated in anger then anguish, then shock, then sadness, betrayal. Utter destruction. Truth be told... the only thing he wanted to do was cry to her... cry to the white bitch... express his emotions to her, for she was the feminine part of him but he couldn't... ofcourse not! He felt like such a simp. Pathetic. He felt like a dog. He felt like he had no value and all of it drained him, and the black concoction of emotions started draining out of him, like blood drains out of a cut wrist and so...

For does the female not become a profound judge for a male? And does a female not become the center of emotion for a male? Why? For a female represents the feminine psyche of a male and so all values are derived from the feminine psyche- ethical, aesthetic, emotional and so, all judgementation arrives from a comparison of the observation with the values ascribed in the tablet the women of the psyche carries in her purse and so in life a male projects all this feminine energy and make his beloved a physical manifestation of this feminine figure that resides in his mind. And so alas... when she degraded him so disrespectfully, with such pretty lies, manipulations, promises- all a seduction that made her enter his spirits and so too did she become his judgementation spirit... oh and then to betray him in such a manner- such a way as to tell him, " you mean absolutely nothing to me. You are not good enough. NO! In Fact, you are not good at all, for you are worthless. I need a real man." And so... by these words that had concocted themselves in his unconscious mind, the lonely dog became The Worthless

Dog, for because she thought him worthless, he thought himself worthless, pathetic and a loser cuck. And so.... The pain burnt within him as now he perceived his own feminine psyche to have betrayed him and so the aggression of the masculine fueled a war within. And there the battle began and the separation of the feminine and masculine started. And thus that angry chief warrior of a man in his head started to murder the feminine, for he couldnt bare to disrespect himself so much as to return to the white bitch, not physically, not mentally. And so.... The rage burned her out of existence and so too all his feminine psychic structure. And thus... he was aroused! No longer a love dog but just: The Dog. A skin of aggression and anger! Yet... now what was he to do, but sit in the sulking of the spicy tears that burned bitter with rage. Ah! The power that he possessed in his testosterone... yet still... ah the incompleteness... the betrayal and ahhh.... she still lived! She still lived in his psyche and the war still drew on. . But what to do.... And here he collapsed upon the grass unable to move in his depression.

Innocence, Femininity & Existentialism

As the feminine represents ethics, morals and values, often a man feels much judgementation from his girl, as she is the physical representation of the feminine. A man often also views his beloved as pure and innocent. And very often when his beloved does something morally hideous, an existential nausea arises within him, often where he has great distortion of his and the world's concept of morals. Thus he is in pain.... A specific type of pain, for there are many different types of pain... this pain we are speaking of specifically is an existential pain and so it has a great feeling of emptiness and confusion directed at the great questions of life- the typical characteristics described of anything existential, such as existential pain, existential depression, existential disgust. This specific pain is not justly described- for that is impossible, as one can only truly appreciate it through direct experience. Perhaps this too is truly necessary for a man. For one must understand both the masculine and feminine energies- those two concepts that are actually impossible to understand, yet nevertheless, are expressed calmly and violently in all humans every single day.... But alas, we do have a grand question in reference to our understanding of masculinity and femininity: is it getting harder to understand? Is the progress of society so divorced from the balance between masculinity and femininity - that balance so necessary to be able to define masculinity and femininity- that it is actually getting harder to understand masculinity and femininity? In the past was there actually a time when people actually understood fully what masculinity and femininity are?

Bitches... Bitches... Bitches...

"We a haven't seen you in a while. And we were a wondering what in the hell has a happened to you?"

"And we was a right to look for you! Look at this lad. What's a gotten into you?"

"The saddest thing is she hasn't even come to look for me and even sadder is that I want her too. How pathetic Am I?" And then he muttered quietly, "I hate myself."

"But don't worry. He doesn't a love her and he wont a love her."

"No. No. No. Don't you see! That makes it even worse. Is all my love made in vain? And we didn't even make love. Is that it? She didn't let me."

"Boy, imma tell you something. U can't love a bitch. Even humans know that!"

"And a she... that white bitch- she a real bitch!"

"A wild bitch."

"And boy, you a did dumb to chase a bitch."

"To put it in you humanly perspective, natural dogs are a like men, we know not to chase after bitches, for they are the embodiment of trouble. A man has enough trouble and responsibilities as it is, he doesn't need the disruptions of facades and stupidity. Only boys- those humans who a lack any of them ambitions so central to being a man are so free from responsibilities that they are able to be a seduced by the illogical drama of bitches. And same goes for us a natural dogs, for there is a reason those peculiar feminine beings are called by the name of our peculiar females."

"And us two are always a watching the streets- we know much of what is going on between the houses and the industry. Real men are either trying intentionally to fix the world or make it worse. Boys and bitches are not necessarily bad, some are a intentionally good, yet no matter what their intentions, they are simply too stupid or irresponsible to do anything but make this a here world a worse place. On a mass scale, they are a so toxic, the intentionally bad men and women are excessively envious of their progress into the realms of destruction."

"You don't mean that, though, do you?" Asked the lonely dog.

"Oh I a do!"

"I mean, do you really mean that the real men and women are focused on making the world a worse place?" The lonely dog now stopped his tears, as a new found awe distracted.

"Well it a depends boy… depends on what you define as being real. If you mean they are moral, then no, but if you a mean responsible, then yes. However, remember that no one is innocent anymore. Everyone has a drank the poisonous coolaid manufactured by that absurd factory we call society."

"Well you a see boy, ever since people got the ideas that morals are subjective, they have gotten it all topsy turvy. And I cannot lie... there is not argument against them. That is the problem of a society based a purely on logic. Logically, you can prove anything."

"Yeah. you a see... they make arguments to cater to their desires and all of a sudden everything is moral."

"Shhhh... let a me a speak brotha, imma try and do a bit of that philosophizin and shit. You see, society is based today only on reason- and thus, every in every argument, the premises are assumed to be a true. And you have to... or else, you shall be questioning the premises to your argument forever. And that is the paradox of logic. Logic cannot be the starting point... but alas... man has forgotten about all else... forgotten about religion...forgotten about intuition... forgotten about emotion... and so, man has made an argument for everything in their desire to be acceptable. So when you ask... about good or bad... well, us animals are not all about that subjective morality... but to humans... there is no such thing as good and evil and so... thats a why you see such a society. So alas... we know what is morally wrong, for we are natural and thus objective... but them humans a know nothin about right or wrong anymore. They a hold nothing sacred. Not life. Not love. But perhaps maybe one thing is a sacred to them: appearance. "

"You see, its a funny the things we see and hear."

"Yeah... tell him about what we a heard from the schoolboy on old Mavis road."

"Oh yeah... that was a crazy thing. Man, he was a telling his friend in the most maddened annoyance. Apparently, he was a working on a group project, and you see, this boy was a complaining about people not doing their things a right to him and he told him to bring it up in the next meeting... and what do you know, he does."

"Yeah... so brotha... a what is wrong with that?"

"Ho Ho... imma glad you asked... For he didn't just bring it up, he said: oh, well isn't there something you want to tell everyone? And so, this man... this man, who didn't have any complaints was all of a sudden placed in such a place ot deliver the complaints of this other boy here."

"Oh and I will a tell you... if that was a me, I wouldda been a mad like that there Madhatter."

"Yeah and so, you a see... these boys... these boys."

"Brotha... let me explain it to a him... You a see... He is a shy boy who pretends to be confident.

"Yeah and remember a here boy! Every time someone talks of confidence, you know they are just a boy- for confidence doesn't exist- but is just a facade. But a continue my brotha."

"Yeah. you a see, this a boy here shall force men to do socially hard things- by that I mean, he makes the confident man look bad. One can think it is bad taste to befriend him. It is his vanity that he cares about so much. And it is this vanity that makes him lose friends. For protecting his vanity destroys his vanity. That is the seed of deceit. And here in human society it has grown like a pimple... swollen and juicy- ready to a pop! Ahhh. I would a say- never trust those who try to look good. But perhaps better advice is not to think about looks, but that too is flawed, for one shall look in the mirror. But best of all is a balance... yet that is a too complicated, is it not? Indeed, how complex life is. Ha!"

"What a coward? Or what a crook? Perhaps cowards are a truly the worst crooks. But deceit is always bad."

"Oh ha. In such pathetic petty, even dogs are amused!"

"You see, we a dogs on the street- we dont a run away from humans because we are afraid of them, but because we are a afraid to catch their stupidity."

"Yeah... just a how you were afraid to catch the stupidity of the gardener and a dropped you fish."

The lonely dog smiled at this remark.

"But you a listen here boy. We arn't even done with telling you the whole lot of what we a witness on here streets, or them streets just yonder. But how can we a tell you all that we a seen- for there are simply too many scenes up in here rich ghetto."

"Nah nah. My brotha, we cannot possibly... but we a told him about this here boy. But a here, tell him about thus here girl... that girl who a lead on the guys."

"Which one?"

"Oh yeah... you a see. We a see this all the time. In fact. Lemme just tell you a generalization of them all. And then too, let me a tell you of another boy, we see all too often."

"What boy are you a talkin about?"

"Oh. the type of a boy, who will do anything in front of a girl. A boy so fake... and so fabricated. And so too often those boys shall then talk with the "bros" like they are all too cool, when really they are controlled by their vanity... they are completely controlled by women."

"Oh yeah... Actually let me a tell him of that... but first a tell him about them funky bitches."

"Yeah... them funky bitches... you a see...once again, we can take it to the extreme and a talk about morals... but let us simplify it all a now and say in all simplicity that they have no morals. And it is all too often the case that these same girly girls complain of being some sort of victim of the megaplot by the mega nihilist Mr. Satan himself. Oh... and how much they gossip. And how much they turn everything to their favor. And how much they lie. And I a tell you... I a see it all in front of me and then I hear the same thing from them and you see... everything is a twisted. And don't be a mistaken here- it is not

just them girls, who concoct such fabrications- but too their are boys on the streets, who are very much indistinguishable from bitches- in fact, I'm a here worried, their fallaces might a start growing in reverse direction... but alas, I shall suspend my opinion and keep everything to one thing at a time."
"Brotha... brotha... you see. I a just had a realization... they are all the same person... they are all simply just bitches. No matter whether they are male or female... all these fellas we are describing are exactly the same. They are bitches."
"Yes... yes... indeed. I cannot see a difference in them whatsoever. But alas... I think we can now give you these final analogies and you shall finally understand what a bitch is. So alas, I shall a restart my first analogy, then I shall tell you of the bitch boy and then I shall finally end to you with the great fight. Oh yes, that great fight... where everyone had skewed their views an so had such gossip been passed around that the men who are in their rights are turned to demons by those same demons who are in the wrong... oh and we a here... us two simple animals laugh at all this fiction... for how blurred them lines have become... I a tell you... I shall laugh as I tell you of this here great fight. HA AH!"
"Oh brotha... these bitches are really foolish, eh?"
"Alright. Alright." And the lonely dog cut in. "You dogs are terrible... I am here dying in suspense and you guys are just yippin and yappin. Get on with it I tell you!"

"Oh you see though my friend, the best way to capture someones attention is in suspension and you see my a brethren, you in definite need of to be in suspension of our tales."

"And you a see brotha, he aint a sad anymore... he is... he is a curious now. "

Yeah. Brotha, let us nt torture him any longer, but a first, i a must say: we are simply genius. Absolutely stupendous with our intelligence. We are indeed what them brits a call, "the dogs bollocks," but holla holla, we a really the dogs."

"And not just any dogs, we are : THE DOGS!"

And the two brothers howled in their ecstasies.

"Alright. Alright. We get it. You guys are clever. Now get on with it!"

"Oh yes... where shall I begin? Yes... have you not seen the girl who pretends to be faithful, staring at a man and unmasking that blissful ignorance- for all of seduction is the unmasking of the innocent ignorance to display the face of possibility. But yet, such a women go further and flirtatiously deskin the face until the point of desire- and then. A once a man's heart smiles at the thought of her, her job is almost complete, for she has one final task: to reject him while scowling, "I have a boyfriend, how much of a creep you are!"

"Oufff... that is simply a heart wrenching brotha... and... And how often has she forgotten about her "boyfriend" herself? How often has she mentioned him? How often has she betrayed him? Yet, God forbid that she is in the wrong, for she is always the innocent victim. And one wonders and asks, why has she behaved like so? Why? Sometimes it is intentional and sometimes a girl is simply too stupid. Or perhaps she pretends to be stupid. But that is the fashion of society: animalistic. "

"Attention whore. She doesn't really love her boyfriend, but uses him simply as an instrument of status. But alas, that isn't enough- only when she has the attention of everyone, especially those who her boyfriend wouldn't approve of giving attention to her- that is the real prize for those a bitches. But are they are too stupid to see how false all this here attention is… how inorganic… how pathetic… haha.. It a makes me here laugh. Funny bitches!"

"Funny bitches! Ha Ha."

"And now, perhaps I have a promised you to give you more details, but I too am a ripe bitch, so forgive me dear friend, but alas, I a think you got the point. Bitches are bitches and so too are you and we. Let us not ponder anymore over these analogies."

"Yeah… a yeah. Really, there is nothing much of it. Bitches are bitches. The end."

"But what about the fight? I wanted to hear about that!" And that curious agitation sivered through the lonely dog.

"Oh look a hear boy. Its a simple case. These to boys fought over a bitch. They a both liked her and she a liked them both and a so, they both had a brawl on the street. Yet, it being said so, everyone made their own fairytale. At first, it was just a yelling at each other, even though both of them boys were truly innocent and yet only that girl was to blame, for she pulled a double dip on them boys. And alas, so they started on the street corner, by the old corner store, a over by the tracks. From the yelling, a punch began to fly and then another and soon, a siren and some blue lights broke off the fight. But alas, for the next week we be a hearing all sorts of fairytales. A one said, the other came and tried to a tickle his pickles. And another squad up here said that their buddy was attacked, when actually it was exactly their friend who had set the first blow. And the cheers and hoorahs the befell upon the nights, when one squad a says that their friend had won the fight- when a we here two brothas saw the fight and we can positively say: a nah! He was the first to have bean toppled to the ground. And so, even through all this stupidity, we hear all sorts of slander too. I a hear one squad say that the boy from the other side was harassing a women, when a really, we a know him- he was a really helping his old granny. I don't a really wanna get more into it, but you can see alas… it is all deceit layered upon stupidity. And so too, we must a say, the boy who got attacked was really not even a tryna fight, but then he gets a blamed for everything and a soo too, we a hear irrelevant people- people who a have here nothing to do with the fight spit a bad word on his name. And so, just over a nothing, but being blindsided by them bitches, his a whole reputation be a taken from him."

"And brotha, you a know what really gets a me? Why we a never hear a thing bad, about the bitch who had actually caused the issue."

"Yeah. And also too. I a hate how she a actin all innocent. Tryna act a all so sweet, when she a knows real well what she had a done. That a actually woulda made me a mad… but how so can we expect anything to befall upon the most innocent of bitches?"
"And also there are those who know what is right and wrong but out of fear of judgment, they take the side of the wrong and manufacture a dirty belief upon the pure. They don't just stay silent, but even actively slander. That's the weakest shit i've ever seen. Thats some real bitch behavior. How vain? Never trust people who gossip vainly, for they are certainly class 5 bitches."

"Alas. This is why I decided to stop telling you of it all... for now we have already concluded our hypothesis: bitches are bitches. No need to pursue further evidence."
"Everything wrong is due to them bitches now... indeed."
"Yeah... so don't be stuck up by them bitches. "

"You see too, them bitch boys too are to blame for bitch girls; just like bitch girls are responsible for bitch boys. These a here bitches think they can get away with anything and everything- but this is the fault of the other bitches surrounding the main bitch causing them issues."
"As a they say... birds of a feather flock together."
"Yeah, a next time you find yourself afflicted by personages unfavourable, think: if I am affected by bad people, then how bad am I?"

The dogs, then stopped for a moment.
"Oh bitches... bitches... bitches. Funny bitches. Funky bitches."
The assassin dogs sniggered.

"And a you too: don't be a bitch, lil boy." One of them warned the lonely dog and then returned to his brother. "Oh brotha... it would a suck to be a human... for they have much more stupidity to deal with. I don't think it is possible to maneuver correctly, even with all the sagacity of a man. So, he is often in a position where he must be at ease with his judgementation.

"But alas, are all men and all women not sometimes bitches in this modern day and age?"

"Oh indeed... so thus, men and women, must always be easy with bitches, for they know they are all too similar. Wow. the troubles of being a human... alas, I am grateful for being a dog."

"Yes me too... well, we can learn something from them humans tho: let the past be the past."

Oh indeed brother, that is a valuable lesson... and so fundamental to the human species, for if the past is not forgotten, then every human alive today shall remain a bitch for perpetuity! Wow. Alas... The past is the past."

Now they turned back to the lonely dog, "you see, what has occured to you is normal. It is no big deal. So don't a fret about it."

"But... but, a brotha... he was in love."

"Ah... love... such a human he is. You a see, you a never fall in love with a bitch. That is just not what you do. But you are all too human, so of course you had a fallen in love with a bitch. If you a really want her, you must defeat the alpha. That is simply the nature of wild dogs."

"Yeah, only the alpha is able to love… not that he does… but he is hypothetically able to. So if you want to a love- you must a defeat him. Kill him. Eat a his guts for breakfast. Ha Ha!"

"Yeah us a dogs here are more simple. We just live for the pleasure. We are simply pimps. So we don;t know what it is about love that a tickles your fancy. We simply accept our beta position."

"Yes indeed. We love to be beta. We just a sleep around and bully em cats. Naturally, us dogs would a be aggressive and active, but out a here, all us dogs have a grown a fat off a trash.

"And us gangstas are still a fit, for we a hump and play, for we are still a young and horny. Yet see the alpha- he is a fat and ripe to be taken out. He hasn't fought for ages now, for life is good in his kingdom. He too use to be a monster and he could prolly still topple a trash can- I mean, the large ones. He can a prolly still murder us fools in cold blood. But look! He a lies in the grass and is obviously not good in bed."

"And is that not all of society in one place? Laziness, power, sex and bitches. He is a paradox. He is not fit for wild life. But we are in society now- ever since you humans have setup this village on our turf."

"Oh the alpha! You are disgusted by him, yet you respect him. You want to be nothing like him, yet you crave to be him. That bastard!"

"Yeah... a yeah! And he a doesn't love either, for wild dogs don't love. You domesticated pet, you. You can surely take him in his sleep if you were to maneuver cleverly, for he a sleeps a slumber- a sin in the wild, for he knows all us dogs in the suburbs are too lazy to challenge him and you are simply too innocent. So thus, I know you shant do what I a tell you, but it was at least a fun conversation, ha, ha."

And with that, the two dogs nodded at each other and began to walk off, "Take care lil one. We are off on important business. A see ya soon."
The other dog blew a kiss at sparkles and then they were gone.

Horny for Murder

Imagine...

Imagine living in a shell... a shell so desolate, that even your skin tries to suffocate you. Forever more this dog... this lonely... this abandoned... this betrayed... this horny dog went... he kept seeing... smelling... hearing of all the betrayals of this world. He would constantly hear the moans and howls of the white bitch, for she had become the alphas' new toy. Worst of all... or perhaps not... for when in such a state of mind, who can possibly say what is the worst part of the emotional rot that stews up in the chambers of the heart? Who can sort what is worse, the moths' larvae pulsing in your stomach or the maggots eating at your brain and so... what is worse? Who knows, but perhaps... perhaps the worst thing was how utterly careless the alpha was about her... so little did he even talk to her... and how much our confusedly vile hero now was, for he imagined how gracefully he would have treated her... how much love he had for her and so how this whole exposition betrayed the concept of love- it added to the severity of the betrayal! And how questions kept rupturing to it all. The whole plethora of unanswered questions. The rage it built up was astronomical.

And then on the other side, he kept seeing Lassie with her boytoy, always showing him off to everyone who she encountered with such pride... such was it that it caused him to reminisce... but not in melancholy: no! But in sadly maddened pain! Oh! And she saw him. And she didn't dare look twice. And so... his jealousy grew into a consuming fit of torment that bubbled- for he was now beyond having want for her... but rather wanted to annihilate her... he no longer felt able to be good as hate has now consumed him in its totality! She didn't even respect him enough to smile... even with her eyes... not even her lips. Damn! And so... how can someone take such disgrace as the abandonment of a mother to someone else... someone who he also didn't comprehend. In fact in such a case, for the boyfriend had treated him nicely, he wanted to hate him but logically knew he couldn't and this doubled down on his anger at both him and Lassie.... Oh the anger! The heat of it! It swelled and consumed. And so days after days! DAY AFTER DAY! He could no longer accept himself to the slavery of circumstances and it all finally exploded... all of him exploded. His ego enrolled upon the identity of destruction: anarchy to these beings! So upon it did he now become: horny for murder! Horny to kill. To taste the blood of his enemies. To take vengeance of these cruel bitches who had tormented him... perhaps to be the crude right hand of justice... or perhaps to be evil. But nevertheless... for when you reach certainty in your intentions you don't care about reasoning, but are rather pumped by the emotions, like toxins through your blood, you reach the heart of your reasoning and declare the verdict! And so... this dog had no longer a care in the world, but all the rage of one who cares about everything. Ah! The Violence of arousal now strikes through him. He had declared his decree. And so... he was horny for murder. HORNY FOR MURDER!

The only lust left in him was for blood... for how sexually gratifying is the sight of blood... not any blood... but the blood of your enemies upom your tongue... that warm blood mixing with your cold hearted saliva... HAH! Yes. Indeed there are only two things which feel as good as sex. Sex itself and Murder! And alas... this horny, lonely, enraged bastard son of a bitch was: HORNY FOR MURDER.

Vermillion

In the calm of the winter night, as all the dogs chilled, wrapped in their own skins, grasping their last warmth, their stood one dog, warmed by his rage- the rage of history- that history which burns through a man's blood, that rage which is the cosmic rage felt by men from the beginning of time... that rage that now engulfed and suffocated. And it is this rage that is the rage of all a man's tragedy- that is the history- a non stop tragedy, where within lieth those brief moments of relief which serve as nothing other than a little sugar to amplify the heat... amplify the pain... amplify the spice of anger. And here... here stode the lonely dog, no longer lonely, for he was now accompanied by the devil and his sulfurous words: the words of conviction- the negotiation of consciousness- the reasoning- the justification- the emotions- the memories- the betrayal and oh- the identity. Yes. The identity- that idea which is the great clash between nothingness and greatness; what a magnanimous pseudo realization: you must be the alpha! For how else can you possibly justify yourself as something worthy of a life? And thus, is it not clear that the lonely dog was really the lonely human, for what other creature could justify such an entertainment of their dark side? And here lies his target, perched, rolled into a ball in the grass. "The fat dog." And here with the inferiority-superiority complexion of jealousy that raged through the shell of his identity into the tempest of his biology grew the passion swelling inside him ever greatly with each step... yellow... orange... red... Vermillion!

Vermillion... Vermillion emotion. Villainous compassion. Vermillion jaws in the villainous throat. And: Vermillion! As his jaws ruptured the throat of the alpha, a squak was heard, a rattle and a tattle as he squimes upon the ground, half mixed in the utter feeling of suprize yet acclaimed terror. His eyes shot open. His nasal hissed. But Vermillion! VERMILLION. The liquid ruptured through, oozing out the jaws of the angry dog... the jealous dog... The Vermillion Dog. And so the deed was done... but no! With each squirm, each floundering flutter... he bit harder and harder... this was no longer a mission, this was a murder of passion. Vermillion passion.

And he could taste the vermillion. he could hear the vermillion. He could see the vermillion. He became the vermillion. The horrid, wretched vermillion. The vermillion intoxicated by the power of lust and the lust of power- vermillion emotion of anger, hate, jealousy, pain, pleasure, suffering, hierarchy, identity and it all contracted into the beauty of an ugly passion: Vermillion passion.

And so now that the alpha was dead, his rage burnt stronger and stronger and so there she was: The White Bitch.

And with all that vermillion that boiled in his blood, he looked upon her and then the rest of the dogs in such ferocity. And everyone could taste their visions, as the flavor oozed and soaked their tongues, marinating their brain into the new reality: but what was this taste? Vermillion! That was the taste. And with his looks he prevented any of the observers from being shocked by affirming that there was a new reign upon them: The Vermillion Reign. And so he looked back upon the white bitch and now decided that it was time to conduct his first order as alpha and mounted her. And in such aggression, he lacked any care, any love but out of pure vermillion he mated with her over the dead corpse. In such mating he was so brutal, so lacking in any care of her, it was borderline rape apart from the fact that she didnt only let him, she promoted it and for she could feel his power, she enjoyed the pain, and enjoyed the utter digust he had for her.

The fact that the violence, the abuse, the disregard for any affection, the stature, the power- all that is vermillion. The fact that the vermillion turned her on and induced more joy than anything else is evidence enough that there is indeed something so wrong... the vermilliin that murders is the vermilliin of pleasure. VERMILLION.

Vermillion
Vermillion!

VERMILLION!

How this emotion runs through the veins of society and suffocates. And it now becomes evident why sex and violence and love and greed and resentment and pain and beauty and jealousy and insecurity and confidence all relate: it is through the vermillion. The vermillion emotion left to rot the brain by running through the blood. It is this vermillion that lacerates and decapitates all morals. And it is this vermillion that breeds an arrogance- and what type of arrogance shall we say it breeds? The arrogance of aggression- the arrogance of action. For is arrogance not a covering up of the deepening insecurities of man? Is arrogance not a form of concealing that vermillion blood? But indeed in all its attempts to close up the doors to that hot vermillion- the vermillion still enters the mind, for the vermillion was always in the house of the heart. And this vermillion is the underlying mood of society, despite all of man's efforts to veil this animalistic energy in the veil of sophistication, the vermillion still remains deep within- so deep that that sophistication is really the vermillion in disguise. And so... with each angry movement, the vermillion dog became more and more suffocated by the vermillion, until he was finished. And it seemed that when he came, he came to his senses... not right away, but soon as he had finished, he looked upon the seen with the angry clenched jaws, that battled the euphoria that now ran through him and now stood back, looking more and more upon everything, while slowly inching away. And thus he had that realization: he had accomplished everything he wanted. He had gotten power! He had received power and so... he didn't know what to do... and so this vermillion seemed to change form and became a confusion and thus as he began to move backwards his pace quickened and quickened and then turned around and began to run. And as he ran, he began to cry.

Now we may ask, when did this dog lose his innocence? Was it when he committed murder? Was it when he had sex? Was it when he ran away? Or was it before? When the vermillion began to reach into him from the cruel world? Was it when he was abandoned? Was it when he found the white bitch with the alpha? Was it when he stole the fish? Or was it the moment he was born? Born into a world and in such circumstances that it was inevitable that he would become a killer? Or did he ever even have any innocence? For does one not need to have power in the first place and show that they don't use their power in the wrong to declare that they are innocent? Is it not that the weak pretend to be innocent to cover up their weakness? Or is it that he is still innocent?
But alas... why did he run? Why did he run so far away? Far into the distance that no one was able to find him afterwards...

He had not lost his innocence, for he never had it and shall never have it, for what he did had abolished his ability to have it; the future state is an aggregation of the past. You see it takes a certain level of intelligence to be innocent: the acting of innocence without intelligence is only naivete. Yet most intelligent people lack innocence, for maintaining innocence is far too hard, for when one has corrupted their conscience, then they have learnt the importance of goodness and thus only then can they truly appreciate innocence.

What is the Vermillion?

As one advances towards pleasures, they advance away from happiness. For happiness is the simple gaieties, while vermillion is the fancy pleasures. Vermillion is the pleasure of power, unaffectionate love, hierarchy, dominance and all the things when consciously seeked lead to destruction and violence. It is exactly this vermillion which is unfortunately what modern society is built upon- covered up in the disguise of sophistication.

All is vanity! That vanity is the socially acceptable means for expressing the vermillion. It is often a possibility to even cover up yhe most saturated vermillion in sophistication, such as murder converted to honor- a common tactic when two countries declare war over silly issues: that is the power of vanity! And so vanity is so prevalent in society for modern man's blood is vermillion; modern woman's blood is vermillion. Vermillion pumps through the sewers and the golden cammodes and the caviar and it rests in the handbag and in the crack pipe and in the classroom and in the courts and in office and in the park and on the walls: everywhere is vermillion. The city is vermillion. The people are vermillion. The atmosphere is vermillion. And thus is society broken... for society is vermillion.

Chap: Proof he is not arrogant

The vermillion dog tried to kill himself again... in fact, he tried 3 times, but with no avail and so he realized he had to suffer the pain of the vermillion. And perhaps this is an indication that he was still innocent? But alas, he could feel the vermillion energy drench into him killing him from the inside- this was different vermillion though- for as we have seen the vermillion likes to shapeshift and now this vermillion was an angry guilt- an exasperation of trauma... oh vermillion suffering- a crisis. A crisis of achievement.... The crisis of power of status... all a destruction of the true individual as for one follows into the deluded path of the social order. And so, we must realize how now, this dog sat with the grasses upon a quiet lonely beach somewhere far away dealing with the inner world.

And now the vermillion dog accepted that he was a dog... a vile creature... he was a wild dog. And so he realized the sad reality of it all and became a solitary dog again, fishing upon the beach and trying to heal and yet still even with this acceptance of it all, he still couldn't help but think he...think there was... some means of healing. Confused and confused he strayed into this new life of his, embarrassed by his outer self and disturbed by his inner self. Perhaps that is what you call a broken heart.

And guilt… oh… despite the acceptance of society to his actions, he knew of its terror and so… so… he was guilty. Deep guilt. Dark blue guilt… that same guilt of the blue baboon… for perhaps to become innocent, one must first be guilty- oh that is probably rubbish- but perhaps in this there is a conception to appreciate, where through the suffering of guilt can one understand evil and can one understand the world. And through this experience can one perhaps sympathize more and judge less… but alas… to this guilty dog, he recognized the evil within and he knew he was guilty. And yet, it first bothered him profoundly- and so he had endleslly meandere through the dark realms of his mind and through his heart contemplating suicide, yet… no avail. And so the guilty dog still on certain occasions felt the incisions of his memories upon his entrails and he would suffocate under tearful words of sorrow… but alas, no avail. He had reached a point of acceptance… acceptance of his crude self and here he loathed himself with bitter self-deprecatory hatred. Oh he had never been loved truly and now…NOW: it was clear. And so, he learnt from his experience that he couldn't be loved and thus abandoned loving himself. And so, thus he became: The Sad Dog.

The nature of some thoughts

Does not one understand the hatred of himself more than the hatred of anything else? Or perhaps least of all? And perhaps one says: I hate things in others, which I subconsciously hate about myself? And perhaps that is something which only people who don't hate themselves have to say. And despite acceptance of the cruel fate of this dog, that chaotic mistress still occasionally strokes at the foreskin of his heart... oh indeed.... For one often in such moments of destruction adds gas to the fire of his anxiety by thinking they should be cured... but time is... as we have discussed: an incomprehensible component of life.
And how pathetic he feels!
And how much of a dog he feels... no... not a dog, for dogs are too smart to love... no... he felt... he felt: pathetic.
A loser.
Oh. And angry. And embarrassed. But mostly: sad.
Of sadness poured upon the sad dog. But what is sadness?
Oh...

And now that all was done, he wondered about ethics... oh how did he know anything about ethics? He assumed there was an ethical framework within him and despite the ethics of the dog world, he knew his to be correct... correct to him at least. An ethics which was pure- an ethics that kept white with the purity, rather than a bloody ethics of vermillion. Oh but... what a devastation... Perhaps his ethics were broken! But how.... How could he just... kill... is dog supposed to be so...

And here arose the worst question ever: shall a man be nice? Shall a man be nice even though he is abused? Even though society respects those who are aggressive, conniving, immoral- yes even in the question of what is morally right and wrong, there are things which are immoral- not wrong: but immoral! And what is it! This power! This thing! This idea to be the leader of the pack. This so-called risk. And now did everything not degenerate back to sex. Sex that insisant force of nature that makes man insane! That idea that holding on to purity is so painful. But why? Why? Why is it that the pure are disrespected? Why is it that the pure are not appreciated? Why is it that arrogance is a fashion? Why is it that people are attracted to those who don't love them? Why is it that everyone seems broken? Where has the purity gone? Why is it that people say nice guys finish last? Stereotypes all too often emerge from underlying patterns! So perhaps all is a lie, but how often is there truth within a lie; how often is there lie within truth.

Oh? So what shall a man do? Shall he turn vermillion? Or shall he be as lonely as the white? Complete with all colors, but in such complete purity is he alone. Oh. For this was the impossibility of his thought?

How shall one act?

He tried the vermillion and he thought about purity and he realized that they both sucked? But what shall he do?

Oh... and it all boils down to sex.. people for some reason dont appreciate the magnitude of sex as a driving force in society, and so a man like Freud has a bad name, yet is it not now obvious that sex is such a broken conception in society. Oh are animals not given value in the herd by sex? And vermillion! That loveless bastard is animalistic. The animalistic drive that has no appreciation for anything as human as love, but is simply the drive of animalism... a sight which is orderly in the animal kingdom- but to humans? To humans it is antithetical to their nature? But indeed have humans not always been antithetical to their nature? For the nature of a human being is a nature that is a paradox. Oh humans! Oh society? Oh how u have destroyed the good? Oh and now upon the shrubs and the sand, the sad dog sat and wished he hadn't gone towards the vermillion, but alas... the rage started burning up again. The heated sexuality... and oh... the vermillion rose up and made him proud.... But then he cried: "NO!"

What a devastation he was. And so, cognitive dissonance arose within the neurons of his entire body and: Ahh! The pain! The immense suffering of his self. The totality of him was destroyed and so... he now sat, empty minded and awed by the satisfactory realization that he hated himself.

Ah he hated the vermillion. But how unfair was it to be in the white? Ahhh.... White like the white bitch... that bitch... she was a real bitch and finally the anger of his hatred broke him into a bit of clarity. Ahhh. How much he hated life. How unfair. And remember he was a murderer by his own accounts, he had slept with her, but how much he hated this reality. How much he now hated sex. How much he now hated everything resembling hierarchy. And he thought: well do the vermillions feel love- but alas- the bitch Lassie was in love.* Oh! How much he wanted karma, despite the fact that he would be ruined... he at least thought that he would find solace in society being just: but no! Did karma exist? He didn't know? This lonely dog, he knew there was hell and heaven, but so too did he wish for his enemies to go to heaven and his friends, but alas... for he was still pure. But innocent? No. He wasn't innocent and he begged the lord to forgive him.

*Was she?

And so… is it that perhaps the nicest people are those who have been most evil before? No! For life is a mixed batch. And so too do those who have repented revert back to sin. And there was solace in God for him and so he relaxed.

Imagine if he was an atheist?

Imagine the torment of the soul to realize that there was nothing fair? Oh. One must appreciate that a society which has lost religion is so unfair. And if he was an atheist, would he not be able to sleep? Would the terror of society not be so immense that he would press the nuclear button? The idea of fairness… haha… something which humans don't have the capacity to appreciate with their self-centered view of life. And appreciate how now this dog was thinking in terms of being a human- why though? Because after feeling like a dog he realized, he was truly a human. Oh… humans… what suffering it takes to be a good human?

Press the nuclear button and erase all humanity, for when was the last time you had met a person who is pure? Forget innocence! That is too much! Innocence no longer exists! It is purity? Simple purity? Where have you gone? Oh purity? For perhaps you have always rarely existed? And was it not only the second generation that had committed the first murder over a woman? Cain killed Abel over a girl and so… again and again… and again… humanity repeats itself over the impossibility of the feminine… and women want to be like

men? Ha! What a joke these modern feminists banter about:
women trying to be like men? What a disgrace it is to all that is
feminine! The feminine is so profound- so powerful- the
masculine fight over the feminine- the man kills for the
woman!
If one appreciates the afterlife, then one appreciates fairness...
but alas... still... oh he was disturbed... and still: he felt pain.
Sometimes the logical mind seems to be unable to control the
emotional mind... or perhaps is emotion not the starting dictum
for all logic?

The Black Lady

One night upon his stroll on the beach, when the tide was low, the sky was clear, the stars bright, his tears black, his heart blue and his vision tunneled into the perplexity that is the confusion he had been too lazy to have. And there lay another dog. And it was a she-dog. The sad dog scoffed, for he was bitter and indeed he truly hated women. Oh. And he continued with his walk, but he did notice something: she was hurt. But why should he care? She was probably just another bitch. And then he wondered: was his mother a bitch? Oh. Probably. How all women are such despicable creatures. But how everyone is despicable. And he continued his stroll.

As he returned to his patch on his sandy hill, he had a realization: wait... let us not expect anything. Let us not befriend her. Let us not get near her. But alas, let us do one thing: let us be pure. Let us catch a fish for her, so she can recover. Let us then avoid all of her... oh how bitter beings are. But alas, we shall do something good for no other reason than doing something good. But wait...
Here again he thought: is it not this idea of doing good simply for the act of being good that which makes people seem weak? Would she not be disgusted and see me simply as someone to be

used? Is it not the act of being good that is so sinful in this dystopian society that we call modern society? Well... who cares what she thinks of me! Who cares! " It's simply: I don't care o'clock right now. I shall do good for God's sake. And if she dislikes me for doing good for her- let it be." And so thus, is it not truly the strong who are able to bear the idea of looking weak?

So, the sad dog found himself upon the water and he waited and waited for perhaps an hour and so, in this time how often did he think that she would have thought of him as a loser- seeing him upon the water for her? He must truly be a desperate loser- are not all people who try to do good for me beneath me? "But this beach is on: I don't care avenue," he said to himself and bore the pain of judgementation, despite how he could feel it upon her eyes lashing at his back. And alas... he decided: I shall never turn to the dark ever again- I shall be strong and allow it all to disintegrate me, but alas... let me be good.

And so finally he caught a fish and to her he took it and thus he laid it down infront of her and he noticed that she was badly scarred all over. He almost felt pity... but ha! No pity shall he give. No emotion shall he show. He simply laid the fish down and turned away without a word and walked away.

"Wait!"

But the sad dog ignored it.

"Wait! Wait! Is this for me?"

And thus he stopped and waited for her to finish- he could hear it already: "you must be some loser to give this to me."

But he did stop and said, "yeah." And then continued his walk.

"Wait! Wait! Thank you. That is so sweet. What's your name?"

And he stopped!

"My name?"

"Yeah. Your name. Thank you. That was so nice of you. What's your name?"

"Its Sparkles." And with that he turned around. "I haven't heard that in a long time. Do you have a name?"

"Yeah, it's Chloe."

"How did you know I had a name?"

"Doesn't everyone?"

"No. Not wild dogs."

"Really?"

"No. And I had forgotten I had a name until now."

"You've been abandoned for long?"

"I was born abandoned. I was only enslaved by different masters and that's where I had gotten my name."

And with that he started walking away.

"Wait! Wait! Come eat with me. It's too much anyway."

"No. Eat the rest later." And he turned away and went back.

The Questions of Hope

Days had gone by and Sparkles and Chloe had talked some more. Infact, eventually over the course of many lunar cycles, they did finally talk. And it is such a case, that us humans often hope for some romance to occur, for perhaps, we wish to have faith in life and often we struggle very harshly to hold onto that constantly fleeting hope. Oh hope! How much we must grasp at it in modern times, for it is always being pulled out from beneath us. It is this hope too that when absent is rather vile. It is this absence of hope which we imagine to be a state so hopeless, so terrifically lethargic: a deep depression of lifelessness. But have we ever experienced loss of hope fully? Is it possible? For when we think we have lost all hope, eventually hope springs from unexpected places- it seems to always return, maybe not quickly, but eventually. Oh how some people have lost hope for years and then finally, it resurges in the most unexpected locations. Oh Hope! And when we lose hope- perhaps it is indeed an ease- for it is this hope- this wantonness for some desire- especially in the ideal of romance, that often drives us to insanity- perhaps we may control it, but somewhere within, its claws sprawl out, ripping at us. Oh hope- what a funny concept! For hope...hope: HOPE! When we lose hope, we lose all fight and we become senile, sterile, inanimate, illegitimatly human. For us humans are in need of that great love, no matter how far we try to run away from it, it is always there, for it is our nature and so, there is no complete annihilation of this hope- this dream. There is only a singular task to undertake: the task of managing the internal and the external, for when the external and internal disagree a deep chaos burns within and a radiation of destruction bursts from our shell and toxifies our fickle skin. Oh and from here we see the colors fade into gray, for that is the matter of the heart: Color. And when the heart begins to fade...

But how, my dear reader, can we possibly manage the violent differences between the internal and the external environments? That seems like an impossibility. It seems even through much meditation, and even through belief in the future- belief being hope transformed in strength to power, for belief is a power- but even so with this belief, which logically we would think to ease us, it so often that our hearts are reigned upon by a tempest of emotions which no logical realization can subdue. Perhaps you may try and control the heart itself, and it seems indeed that that is the best approach, however try and try... and then try again, for in some cases how can the wild dragon be tamed. Oh, the heart is a wild dragon, which is chained by the arms, legs, neck and tail, yet, it is not the one enslaved, for despite that we have tried to chain it, it is simply too powerful and it has reversed the order: it uses those chains to tug at us. We are the ones enslaved by the chains we have connected between us and the heart. You see- you cannot stop the heart from doing what the heart does- repressing it with chains is simply to cause us internal bleeding- for where does the other side of the chain link? The rib cage! And it cracks our bones- we simply cannot repress those emotions, for then our chest is tightened, our body constricted: so we suffocate under it all.

But then what? Allow the heart to go free? Allow the dragon to fly? Oh what a danger that is! Now you understand that there is no escaping the heart, for how can one let the dragon fly and not suffer? Unless the dragon is smart and avoids flying into the abyss above. But how often is the heart smart? Perhaps that is what one must train in- to develop intelligence in their emotions, but how shall one do that? I do not know, for the matters of the heart, are uncertain- illogical- emotional. Perhaps we can train it to be smarter; perhaps we do train it to be smarter. Yet, there is always a glimmer of flaw throughout every human experience- remember time is long- and thus, we will make many mistakes with the heart.

And now dear reader, I believe you understand the great issue of the heart: there is no escape from the suffering it brings about us. There is no escape from sufferings of the heart- whether the heart suffers, or the heart causes you to suffer. But that is life- for life is always dense with suffering.

And, hope or no hope is the same- there is always hope, because the heart always has hope, whether you consciously know it or not.
The only thing we can possibly do now is to understand the heart better- to feel the heart- journey within the chest- listen to the heart, befriend the dragon- visit its chambers and in those chambers shall you find the secrets of the heart. Oh the heart! What a funny thing it is.

Oh so, we can now appreciate the concept of hope and love- a sort of tragedy of humankind. A sort of illness, yet arguably a healthy illness. And so we must ask... well, there are a lot of questions to ask, but let us stop at one, for here in our story we reach the great question: how can we manage the pain of beauty? Oh for how the beauty hurts... burns.
And so rest assured that these dogs- these humans- these beings with the potential to find love- these creatures did start to interact. And so, perhaps we should have hope... perhaps we should try to hold onto it... but is that not too much to ask? Or perhaps we shouldn't try to hold onto it consciously- or perhaps it is the matter of the heart and it has no place in the brain? But does the mind not function better when both parts- the brain and the heart are in sync? I do not know! And how can anyone know? I do not know. So hold onto your hope, or not, or

don't acknowledge hope. There is always hope. But yet we talk about hope, yet we never criticized it!

But that is perhaps your job. Was it not this hope that caused The Lonely Dog to murder? Or was it the lack of hope that did this? Oh, now once again we see the great divide in hope- for remember there is a great divide is all things- there are no free meals- everything has a tradeoff and so, hope is more complicated now than it seems. How do you think of hope? How to manage this beast?

 Oh the mind- the heart and the brain and the depths of it all. You see my dear readers- this is why there is no escape from suffering. For even in your own heart, you shall find vermillion! And so, look into it all, you shall find humans creatures unable to run away from suffering, for they are unable to run away from themselves and we humans have suffering in the heart. Oh how beauty is painful! Oh and then we have a sufferable society- how unsurprising.

The heart is: suffering!

And so they talked.

Eventually they talked, but how a broken heart can only heal when the tape of disgust is removed. Yet it was never removed... for that is our society... the saddest, blackest of all existence is the missed opportunity of profound love which so often occurs

as one has lost all hope of innocence- and for that reason: who
is still innocent today?
But Chloe- the black lady- she was innocent. And if only
Sparkles knew...
But a heart like his would require repair and so does that weird
dance between two dogs on the beach begin: one representing
the ugly, the other representing beauty... one representing
innocence and one representing experience... one hateful of life,
the other hopeful... melancholy were they both. But upon white
sands and passionate skies... there is a chance... perhaps we
may even be hopeful that things may indeed end nicely... dare I
say, we may hope that things end: beautifully.

The news

Within the cold fogs of late summer, upon the road that curled alongside the beach, where the light hushing of calm waves rolled across the sands of night, two black dogs trotted away and now began to enter the dunes of the seashore. Little by little they approached, as the two dogs that had established an estate upon the beach were twisted upon each other in the burrows of the sand.

"Howdy!"

"What? You sayin, howdy?"

And Sparkles awoke.

"Yeah... yeahh..." and the other dog continued, "don't you remember how we met him. He was a sayin howdy to us, so Imma say it a back now."

"Oh yeah, I a remember."

And now sparkles, awakened in his slumber had now realized what was happening and a gleam of fright had streaked him, but it was exchanged for a cold exhale, and he asked, "you came to kill me?"

"What?"

"Brotha, what is this a boy sayin- why he always on some depressing notes."

"I know, right? Why he always thinkin something dark. No, we didn't a here come to kill ya. We a came here to give you some news."

"Oh. I just thought you had come to kill me, since... well you are the assassins and I ran away. I mean you did warn me that you would maybe have to kill me. And anyway, how did you find me?"

"Ah... you hear him, brotha. How did we find him? We should a kill you just for asking such a ridiculous question- we's a told ya- we the damn best in the business... how did we find ya? Ha," he scoffed.

"Yeah. even if you'd a gone to the moon, we woulda find ya."

"But alas, what a you a worried about... there is no issues a now. In fact, we a wasn't even gonna a look for ya, because us wild dogs don't really perceive this as such a profound thing, but, here, my brotha, he a made a good point- he a said you humans are much too emotional. So yeah, maybe this is a something you'd a care about- so we are here to tell you: congratulations."

"Yeah: congratulations!"

"Yeah, you are now a father."

"Yeah, not that you have to come with us or we a gonna kill you, we a just here to let you know."

"Wait... what? What do you mean, 'I'm a father?'"

"Yeah, we saw them- and I a said- those pups- they a definitely from you. Aint no dog in the wild have that type of brown and white coat- not that I've a seen em. So when I saw those little ones, I thought immediately: yeah, them youglings are definitely a yours. And so we came to ya here to tell ya."

"Yeah. you can a come back and a see em whenever you want. Don't you a worry, ain't nobody going to a kill ya. Funny, you are still our king, by the way. We a told you, no one wants to be the alpha and a surprise , surprise, we a held a meeting and ain't nobody willin to do it, so... I mean, you a made things real hard for us ya know."

"Yeah! Real hard."

"We a now have to do everything- we the two fools that are now taking care of it all, while you out here on some beach. In fact, we a hope you come back- you a better help us out with all this extra work that befalls us. Like we have to meet with the alpha from the pack in the East to discuss the problem of them damn raccoons who are makin a menace between our territories. We a say, you know, we ain't never too good with words- it's a better you go to the meeting, but alas, you a still our boss, so we ain't speakin nothing."

"Oh no. no. no. I don't want to. I hate power. I just want to live peacefully in nature here."

"Oh... boy you a hear him... brotha, I tell you, he always pullin maneuvers."

"Yeah... a yeah... I a told you he couldn't be trusted, the first time we a met him. He's a always been a funky fella."

"Anyway,,, you a leave us busy sir, we a now have to actually do something."

"Imagine- us two dogs doing something."

"Yeah. Imagine that us two have to be responsible now. Like wow. We have to actually make sure there are no problems out here. Oh. But I is a tell you... right now, we are lazy, but if say something is needed of you, don't a think we shant come and take you back. Now you can stay here in the beach, but alas we a tell ya... we will be back. Like if them humans start causing a commotion and we's a need to go to war... I a tell ya... your holiday is over."

"Alright... alright, I will come if you need me. I'll even come right now."

"Oh no no no. you misunderstand us. We a just lik to complain- we a just pullin your tail brotha. But do come to see your pups- it is what the humans like to call: fatherly love."

"Yeah a don't' worry- the alpha's job is meant to be lazy- but yeah, we a might need you sometimes- otherwise, we have got everything under control. Yeah, have you heard of Machiavelli?"

"No. I have not," replied Sparkles.

"Yeah, well, neither have we. we a just sayin, though, that a right now, we a run the pack and it is good that you arn't around, because we can a just tell everyone that you a told us to do this and that and they will a listen to us. So you a just stay and rest here and if we a need ya, we will come and get you. You just chill and relax out here."

"Alright, thank you."

"What a you thanking us for boy! If only you a knew how much fun we a havin. I a mean, we now told everyone to collect all the bones from the trash by the butcher- you a believe it- we have more bones than we a know what to do with. Look a here, my brotha's belly even began to grow- he turnin into a fat boy. And best of all, the whole pack even a thinks it's a your idea."

"What do you a mean fat? Brotha, I just a haven't been to the bathroom yet. And I think you the one actually gettin a fat!"

"Anyway, we shall a leave you to your peace, us two have gotta go back to town, because my brother a here, he getting too fat to run, so we will have a long slow walk ahead of us."

And off the two dogs went in their banter, laughing and cackling on the way back, until they disappeared into the fog.

Bastardhood.

Anger and aggression expanded upon the horizon as the two began mushrooming in their atomic scrimmage:

Lassie: "You made me pregnant and now you leave!"
Curt: "Get an Abortion!"
Lassie: "NO! It's our baby! I love it!"
Curt: "You are pro abortion- go get it!"
Lassie: "No way. How can anyone think it's ok. I feel it. I feel its life within me. I was wrong. It is a crime."
Curt shrugs and rolls his eyes, as he steps into his car and ends with sayin: "Look. Never call me. Ever! I never want to see you again!"
And with that he closed his door and Lassie had time to yell, "Asshole!" as he sped off into the far away distance of an old memory- that memory which would unfortunately likely be relived, over … and over… and over….again.

....
....

And so Sparkles and the black lady set out into town the next morning, for Sparkles' wished to see his children. They walked the coiling roads twisting between the foresty mountains on their right and the white sands and azure waters on their left, as the sun shone behind thin clouds. That fresh morning air was just beginning to stir as they entered town, when a bus was arriving from the outskirts of the region, to this suburban town and then heading deeper into the city, leaving behind hints of diesel fumes, which mixed with the scents of the now fading flora. There was also that autumn dampness that seeped out the ground, dried by the energies of the day. The muds began to either crystalize or stick upon the boots of the citizens, as the ants began to march towards their duties and the coffeeshops now scattered with men in suits, holding bagels and coffee, while children made their walks to school. There was a sort of depression in the atmosphere of the city- something not felt in the nature. This was a sort of frantic rushing, that flushed a sense of tired and anxious redness upon the faces of everyone. And so, here for the first time, the philosopher dog in Sparkles awoken to see the reality of city life: a non ending cycle of exasperated smiles and joyous facades to appear content with the non ending cycles of dissatisfactory reality. A reality, lacking in nature; society, a life forged upon the logical ideal that humanity disagrees with. The morning in the city is always a shock for those from the wild, for in the mornings those arise with disgust, where then they use the nights to fulfill shallow joys in order to overcome the internal anxiety bread by disinterest in life- that disinterest of having a life lacking in adventure- that life which turns man into machine. And so, at each coffee shop they passed, they saw each machine in their suits and ties, lubricating their internals with that brown oil served in paper cups. And so that grand economic cycle keeps churning.

And so, as they entered the neighborhoods of Corktown, the two of them came across a scene- unexpected, but unsurprising.

"You made me pregnant and now you leave!" It was Lassie. And now, the two dogs stopped in their journey and watched from the side, as Lassie and Curt began to argue in their clouds of irate sensations. And so, between the scene and Sparkle's ponderous mind, we may appreciate this scene as perhaps a keen conclusion to the earnest nature of the two. And so throughout the mind of Sparkle's, a stream of earnest thoughts glimmer, which perhaps express the some sort of feelings brought about from the past; often it is that we need a closure to a traumatic story: this was Sparkle's. This was when it was made clear- the very understanding of these two characters. The truth is a horrid expression of some acute perception determined by the dwelling of the lower mind and it is so often that a man tries to cover these glowing embers with a shunning distraction, to not burn the upper portions of the mind in toxicity, and it is so often that doing so is healthy, however in such circumstances, where one is able to finally find answers- to test these interpretations, one may finally be able to lift off the veil of distraction and allow the new found observations to dampen the heat of the coals that smolter the heart. Yes. Finally, through additions of understanding is the internal ambiguity able to be healed- the trauma can conclude- the neurosis can be alleviated. But alas, with such conclusions, does one only reaffirm the truths that they already often knew. One often doesn't wish to judge and so blocks their judgmentation- however, when they do see that they were originally correct, then does one finally grasp the reality of how atrocious everything is. So here... the hunches behind all this deep lying hatred can be confirmed- yet through this confirmation of hunches, from the vast sea of uncertainty, does Sparkles replace hatred with understanding. Which is worse? To hate because of the possibility, or to be neutral due to the knowledge of? Worst of all- the confirmation is that which eliminates the painful ignorance that one wishes they could keep- however once the beginnings of a realization are made, the end needs to be met, in order for the emotional mind to find closure. Perhaps this is an unhealthy thing, yet when new things begin to arise into consciousness, one is shocked and one cannot end the shock until it is certain that there is truth to terror- only then can they appreciate then can they process the tragedy from the end- else they must process the tragedy, alongside the uncertainty- which is more strenuous, for in such circumstances, one doesn't learn and one doesn't knwo exactly what it is that they are processing- yet no matter what the circumstances are, it is of naivete to assume good- however it is exactly this naivete which keeps a man good. However, no matter what, the real calamity is the inescapability from the catastrophe of the mind: no matter what, the mind shall murder itself in cycles, that reach out to the furthest strata of time- that is perhaps what makes the mind a phoenix- an instrument requiring constant rebirth- a renewal of personality- a software upgrade. Yes... here once again, we have an uncertainty of how the mind operates, but alas, perhaps one needs to learn in order to write the code for the next update- however so often is a man overreached in his ambitions to learn the truth and so his strides for the realization of said truth becomes dystopic. Alas, here we have a paradox- but be alieved by the realization, that there is no alleviation from the circumstances of mental torture and the cunning debauchery of the curious mind. Oh... that is further accelerating the problems of society- that so peculiar defection of the lower glands of the mind upon the higher reasonings and too that leaves one with the colossal problem: to manage the mind. To manage the torment. To manage one's behavior. And in such circumstances, one may find themselves morally confused at what to do, at how to think, at how to be. And ofcourse, thus, I cannot be of assistance in guiding anyone to the right, for in the head, the right, the left and down and the up are all doorways to self-destruction. It is often choosing the path of least evil and so, in each circumstance, every door is different. Oh sometimes, reality is too convoluted to penetrate!

And so his realizations begin with: perhaps even the nice are not good. For whatever reason. Cowardice? Vanity? Falsehood? Did he even love her? Did she love him?

And now he speaks, "Get an Abortion!"

And she replies, "NO! It's our baby! I love it!"

And for all that, we see that this is our modern society. How a man pretends to love before it's real; how a woman pretends to love after it is real. That sums up all of sex in the 21st century. In such pathetic petty, even dogs are amused. For to modern humans, nothing is sacred anymore. Not life. Not love. But perhaps maybe one thing is sacred to them: appearance. But appreciate how this man, seemingly so nice, has so little consideration of life and love of his unborn child. Nor of his girlfriend. Nor of anything. He even continues, "You are pro abortion- go get it!"

"No way. How can anyone think it's ok? I feel it. I feel its life within me. I was wrong. It is a crime."

How easy is it for a libertine to change their views when it best suits their needs, or for the sake of drama, aggression, or simply to be heard- for the ego of sloppy people is always trying to be noticed, simply because their own conscience doesn't hear it. Perhaps it is because they have never come up with an original thought of their own, or perhaps because they are driven by nothing other than toxic emotion- by that I mean exaggerated emotion- emotions amplified by the cries of crowding insecurity. And thus it leads to two fundamental questions: what was Lassie's real view on abortion? And has her views changed due to the emotions of real motherhood? Something she perhaps wanted since she had adopted the now abandoned dog?

The minds of some are simply incomprehensible, especially the mind of the insecure and it is unfortunate that too many have become insecure by the sprawling of mad hedonism- the hedonism referred to here being the ideology that consequences don't exist within the actions themselves.

What a world we live in, where now the hot topic of debate is abortion, for how did society reach a place where abortion has become so widespread a concept that it needs to be debated over in such heat? Alright, so there may be uses of abortion, but alas, to reach such a grand status- that status of being the fundamental argument in the media- that which many movements are based over- that concept which people side over- a concept which is no longer debated with scientific stoicism, but rather is a debate where your side determines social judgementation, so brutal upon you that it is no longer objective, but a subjective concept that makes you appear crude and disgusting to many. To reach such a stature, means that the premises to abortion, being that of irresponsible sex is so accepted, that it is not even debated anymore- it is seen as an acceptable thing- it is that hedonism which now arises in society- that hedonism which is destructive- where now due to that hedonism, we have now began debating how to best deal with the issues arising from our socially acceptable insanity. That is our society now. For abortion is a debate on how to deal with our mistakes. Else, the concept of abortion would be less intriguing- say if abortions were simply to save the lives of the mother- of if you talk about a chemical abortion in the form of tablets incase of the very real terrors of rape that occur in the evil streets of our vermillion society. Yes. That is something not too complicated. That is something not included in these debates- for that is a simple case of actual issues occurring in society. But alas, here is a society, which has now convinced the world that sex is a safe, unconsequential behavior. And so, in such inconsequential behavior, Lassie had achieved what she truly dreamed of- not in the right manner, but in the impatient, and unintelligent manner. And so, when things go wrong, the favorite action of society is to assign blame.

But here is the thing, there is a danger in it all. That danger being a special type of stupidity. This type of stupidity is one we see much of in society. The most dangerous form of stupidity is that which arises from thinking. But here lies with the intellectual idiot an ever greater folly. They think that they think, yet, what they think is their thinking, is simply a regurgitation of common fashion.

And who leads the march into the new age? These excessive libertarians of course! For who else is self righteous enough to do so? The libertines have that absurd arrogance where they believe in their own rule- where they think they can rule themselves. If only someone had told them, "if you are not enslaved by your government and culture, you shall be enslaved by pleasure and stupidity."

And these so-called 'modern, progressive folk,' these libertarians have even forgotten the meaning of God. They have used religion as a scapegoat for the reason behind the destruction of society caused by the saem hedonistic mentality that their fathers had. And now, the devil laughs, for he has played you! Ha Ha. His tactic: destroy society by hedonism and then blame the problems on religion, thus removing religion from the minds of the mass man- then the real hedonism can begin! The devil likes to party.

And now to return to our dear Lassie. Are the people who complain most of their problems not usually the people who cause such problems and not even become conscious of it? For is she not the type of person who had played sparkles and not even appreciated how much terror she had thrown to him? And definitely, now she is complaining of her lost love. For she had adored sparkles until someone she had perceived better had come about- but thus we say she adored, for she had never truly loved. And for some other reason, women like these never appreciate the concept of karma- for she had been dealt with how she dealt with others. And a woman like her scowls upon innocent men and infatuates over certain men and is left dry, yet still thinks so highly of herself... for that is the irony of arrogance- one over appreciates themselves to compensate for their insecurities. And in such a manner she curses and cries, "why has this happened to innocent, young me?" But karma... and by karma I don't mean anything metaphysical, but I simply mean: birds of a feather flock together. And that is how these people are... birds who appear pretty, but are truly ugly. For these birds shall do all they will with no appreciation of morals whatsoever, but as soon as someone else does anything, they are quick to jump. Of course this isn't a cuss on all women- but simply on the Lassies of the world. Women, in their malice, tend to harm psychologically- where men harm physically. That is the difference between men and women- they operate on different fields. Woman on the internal; men on the external. So men kill and murder one another- men rob- men steal. Most prisoners are male. Male and female are equally capable of evil- however the man is a simple criminal. On the other hand, you have the Lassie's of the world. A different type of criminal. Then there are the Curts- a simpler criminal, but too, he is a criminal. And then you have the criminal like Sparkles. All criminal, different internal stories. Here we shall focus more on the exaggeration of a type of female criminal: Lassie. For this type of criminal is often not well understood, for they operate on a field much different and harder to outline with statistics. The female mind is different in its operations and so, here we shall go into the depths of Lassie. The crimes of men are easy to understand, the crimes of women are often more complicated.

Hedonism is a very pure and saturated vermillion. Not a hue of vermillion, but opaque vermillion.

Finally, sparkles had found consolation in knowing that both Lassie and Curt were in accordance with his subconscious' perception of their perniciousness. Now it all made sense. Now he was freed from the burden of the unjust scrutiny of himself. Now the karmic cycle had been completed. All understanding had been reached and so Sparkles could finally hate himself for his own malignancy; first the affliction of venom must be healed, before one is able to think to criticize oneself, or else the pain of the bite consumes all mental energies. Now finally, the venom was extracted and so, Sparkles could now breathe easy and finally hate himself justly- hate himself for his and only his own poisons. His own mistakes. And although, the circumstances of all his malevolence had started with Lassie, he finally was calm enough internally to process the pandemonium of his great folly, assigning all blame to himself. Yes- he hated himself! He was still a murderer. But alas... he understood. Understood what? Understood everything. And through this understanding, he found ease and through this

ease he took his first breath of enlightenment and upon this breath he transformed into a human.
A real human.

Lassie

Now that sparkles had transformed into a human, he was finally able to comprehend that mysterious figure: Lassie. Despite our rugged attacks upon Lassie and despite that she truly was a bitch, and despite that we shall not pardon her for her behavior, we can appreciate how she had become such a girl. Here we have the paradox, where one shall appreciate in almost pity for those who become corrupted, while on the other hand, we cannot simply justify all their behavior, for that is not how society works- one cannot live without comprehension of the consequences. However, what we can do is understand how Lassie had become so. And first we must start with her family. Lassie was born a single child in a rich household- the daughter of a plastic surgeon. She was beautiful. She had always been beautiful. And everyone made sure to tell her this. Infact, she was told she was so beautiful, so often, she had grown extremely confidence; confidence is seen as a good thing, however, there is always a tradeoff, for confidence means to lack appreciation for the concept of uncertainty, however I shall say that anyone who lacks this concept cannot possibly be intelligent. And so, we can first understand that she had grown excessively confident, for beauty is one of the most important factors for confidence- how the beautiful are treated better than the ugly! But furthermore, let us also note a very strange concept. When a person is constantly told they are beautiful, they begin to focus solely on beauty. They put beauty at the top of their hierarchy of talents and skills. It is not just beauty that this is done with, it is with any trait- start telling people they are intelligent and see as their appreciation for intelligence increases. But in our case, it was beauty. And so, she had discounted the value of intelligence, for no one had ever complimented her for her intelligence. And so, she didn't value it and so she didn't care to develop it. She only developed her beauty and so, she was forever intellectually a child.

And with such beauty, she perceived herself the desire of every man and in all honesty she was mostly right, for all men thought of her excessively attractive.

And more forth, she was spoilt. She had everything she ever asked for- her father simply couldn't refuse her anything. And because she was attractive, no one would ever tell her off- she had special treatment, especially from boys. Infact, girls secretly hated her in envy, for her beauty intimidated them, infact, it intimidated boys too: it intimidated everyone! It was not just innate beauty, but nurtured too- she was early to the makeup game, and she would wake up earlier than most, in order to go through her elaborate skin care regimen. And she would always buy the nicest clothes. And she would practice her walk, her smile, her laugh, her expressions. She would micromanage every part of her, to make sure she was the most attractive, the most sexy, the most beautiful. Every part of her was catering to the impressing of society. And more forth, she had much social media activity. And on her posts, she too would constantly get attention from everyone, much comments spelled, "your gorgeous." And she had many followers- many who she didn't know, but still they would appreciate her beauty and so she became popular in society. She had clout and glamor and status. And she lived like this, so focused on her beauty that her favorite method to manage the triviality of her other less developed aspects was to further emphasize her mental reasonings upon her beauty. And so the beauty took hold of her entirely and nothing else mattered to her in a person other than their surface: their beauty. This is what her life had led her up to- this entitlement brought about by her extreme and narrow focus upon beauty and the society's excessive appreciation of her beauty.

And alas, therefore, when Sparkles was no longer cute, he was no longer so valuable.

There was one more thing about her and it was her family. Her father too had a simple solution to everything: money. When anything was the issue, he simply fixed it with cash. And so, here she learns one other thing- something similar to Curt: money fixes everything. If only someone told her how false that was- but she would very likely not believe it. And so, with this excessive obsession of beauty and her shallow understanding of money, she had liked Curt for he was rich and handsome. He was older and popular. And so, he was the type of person, who fulfilled her fantasy- a sort of person who had all the social standing to properly display her beauty. He would buy her many things- jewelry and dresses and purses. He was something exotic and rare- imagine: she would date a boy 2 grades above her- to her this made sense, for she perceived herself to be so special- she perceived herself to be above everyone else, for she had always been told so by society. She was beautiful- who could possibly be better than her? And so too, was Curt an expert in dating- he was a womanizer and knew all the tricks- he knew how to hold her attention- he knew that she was an easy and stupid target- he was skilled in acting a cadaver in a coffin and so he was perfect, because he was just as vain as Lassie- everything about him was seeming perfection- nothing was real about him, however he knew how to make himself seem like the most popular, most attractive person out there and so, the relationship would never be met on grounds of truth and honesty, but so what? She was beautiful. And she was stupid. And she could be seduced, for she was too easy to manipulate by her grand insecurities, which arose from her enslavery to beauty. So Curt made himself someone she had to satisfy- for the first time Lassie felt like she wasn't above someone- she felt like Curt was actually someone she needed to impress. And her greatest pleasure was to please Curt, for it made her feel like the sexiest woman alive. And this gave Curt colossal power over her and this made him even more attractive to her. He was not just prince charming, but he was also the most powerful kid in school, no, in the world- and those were the perceptions of young Lassie.

And so we can now understand the whole story once we understand how Lassie was raised to believe in herself in such a manner that she lacked all responsibilities, all intelligence, all ideas of consequences, all perceptions of empathy. She grew up in an environment that made her arrogant and conceited; entitled and demanding; disloyal and enslaved; greedy and jealous; hedonistic and childish- however the best description of her would be: Vermillion.

Her father was almost a good father. There is a fine line between being a good father and an incompetent father; Lassie's father loved her, so he was almost good, however he had never disciplined her, nor raised her with respect to any conservations to the idea of quality in humanity. That lacking, her mind was underdeveloped and she, uneducated in behaviorisms, morals, desires, visions, discipline, patience, humility, shame, ideology- those critical aspects that are meant to be brought to fruition in adolescence from the spurring, swelling of the mental buds being watered by the enactment of correct parenthood through a person's childhood. But so, here is where Mr.Rodriguez failed. This is where the fashion of liberality has failed. For he himself was now unaware of the respect for conservative values and even had he known, modern civilizations spits upon the old and claims its way to be immature and immoral. This civilization innovates many ideas too quickly and much so through emotion- much so through hedonism- much so disguised behind fallacious argumentation- much so swelling with the vermillion underneath. And thus, the all too important balance between conservatism and liberalism is distorted, stretched, broken. And so with it the minds of men and women. And with it the next generation shall further stretch and disrupt it and so on and on... society goes. And is it not funny? The tricks of the collective mind. For there is grand stupidity in much thinking. The most dangerous form of stupidity is that which is disguised as thought. The most dangerous type of stupidity is the stupidity which arises from thinking, for it is stupidity disguised as genius. There is much of this type of stupidity in today's society and thus our society has become excessively socially dysfunctional.

And now... the next generation of bastards are born... and so the cycle shall continue...

And the goggles came off.

And the goggles came off… and Sparkles was confused… wait…
Sparkles… no: that's not my name? Wait… Where am I? Oh no!

"Calm down my friend… calm down…. It's me."
And he sat there looking at the 4 Aliens who looked at him and
then realized: he too was an alien.
"How are you?"
"I'm good, but I just… just… got lost in that simulation. Wow!
That was an experience all right!"
"Yeah, now you understand why we don't want to invade
Earth?"

And the 5 Aliens laughed as their mega-nano-plasmic rocket
boosted them out of our galaxy.

THE END.

And the drugs wore off

"Wow!"

"Did you have the same crazy vision as me?"

"Yeah.... Now I know why aliens won't invade Earth Dude!"

"Yeah bruh... like this skunk pheromone is totally like rad bro!"

Aight.... Enough of this for now- I think I will take a nap, for I have a date with that hot girl Lassie tonight!

THE END

And the dream ended

And she awoke.

"Oh wow! I saw so much of life upon me. My whole life is a lie!"
Shizzered Lassie in her night quiver.

THE END

Your metaverse pack has ended

"Your Metaverse Pack has ended... please recharge to play another game."

"Aw man. I can't believe it. We are out of Ethereum."
"It's alright, I'll ask Mr.Rodriguez if he can give me an advance.
"Wait... isn't Mr.Rodriguez's daughter named Lassie?"
"Yeah I guess so... what an odd coincidence."
"And didn't she have a dog named Sparkles before?"
"Yeah she did."
"And wait a minute... didn't she get pregnant?"
"I think so..."
"And isn't this game made by the company Curt's father owns-the same company the Mr.Rodriguez works at?"
"Ye-eh... that is... very... weird."

THE END.

Woof Woof Woof.

"Woof Woof Wooof."
"Bark. Growl."
"Wa wa woof!"
"Wooooooof?"
"Wa woof woof WOOOOOF!"

"Woof woof indeed."

The end.

One final Question

What do we know about ourselves?
Are any of the characters aware truly of why they do- why they act in certain ways? Did Lassie know why she adopted Sparkles? Why she adopted Sparkles specifically from the shelter and not from the pet store? Is she aware of her vanity? Mostly though: what underlying psychological structures do we- you and I- harbor that we are not aware of? What do we truly know about ourselves?

And how much of our behavior stems from us? How much of it is brought about by the brainwashing of society?

Are each character to blame for their behavior? Or not? How much of their actions are produced through free will?

If their actions are determined, are their actions determined by their character? And is the development of their character produced through free will? And so, if their actions are determined, are they then to blame for not developing their minds and thus their characters in a way that determines correct ethical behavior and actions? Assuming that we have the free will to develop our minds and thus our character. But alas... are actions determined, while development of character free?

Ah, the question of free will and determinism and, thus ofcourse: morals.

Can we even have an answer to these questions?

What one hopes is true

This book is a satire upon the most childish philosophy: the philosophy of the alpha male. A joke of a philosophy concocted by a false understanding of femininity by men who have turned to the dark side of ignorant assumption, rather than true understanding of nature- this has grown into a vast network of stupidity, where fallacious arguments are made- fallacious as they are based on generally accepted yet unsound premises forged from ego-preservational emotions of men.

But one thing which seems impossible to refute or even forget is: nature is cruel!

True, now we have evolved into the new age of the sigma male and so, once again we are at the beginning of a new cycle of mainstream masculine philosophies.... Where shall it go? Let us sit patiently and see.

Notice how vanity produces the facade of masculinity- it is also the vain who are attracted to this facade. No high quality women would be deluded as such- but here we are talking about Lassie- who would obviously be attracted to the Curts of the world.

Often many men make a mistake of judging generally high value women to be "bitchy"- however this is a mistake. The high quality women represented by (Chloe- the black lady dog) should never be confused with the Lassies. Lassies are possessed by vanity and thus they're whole operations are "bitchy." On the other hand, Chloe's test a man's masculinity- i.e. this capacity to handle life- this is an utmost important bio-psychological development for a woman and must be appreciated fully. It can often be frustrating, yet it is in order to make sure fully that the male can fully provide adequacy as a father. Of Course so, women do things men perceive ridiculous, yet these are to make sure a man can manage the great hecticness of the randomness of circumstances a child can produce. And thus we see exactly throughout this book how important a competent father and well intact daily is to produce well developed children. However, due to vanity, this whole biological system has been circumvented and nature has crumbled producing children like Lassie and Curt. Thus we should appreciate this extremely crucial feminine behavior.

Notes:

Now, if we were to replace dog with human- by that I mean every time it says dog, u read human and every time it says human, you read dog, there would make no difference to the story, for now in our progressive age- the grand 21st Century, there really is no distinction between man and his best friend. However, I will admit, I didn't want to say this out, for if one were to replace the word human and dog, it would truly be a great disrespect to all canines.

It is a man's plight to go through rock bottom to individuate into a man. Often a man must go through immense stress and then have a break, where the mind can then fit the pieces of the puzzle together- it is his two staged process- contraction and rarefaction- that develops the man from the boy. It is not necessarily something sexual, yet it is this two step process of development which perpetually works man through his stages of maturity, each time leveling him up in any domains that he has planted roots in- such as his love life, his career, his physical body(muscles follow the same pattern)- this is one of the fundamental shapes that nature takes: the shape of waves: rarefractions and contractions.

Idea: as now, physicist theorize everything to be energy- waves, thus do the shapes of waves flow from the quantum to the ordinary world? How? I have no idea! Perhaps it is just a coincidence.

 Notice the characters in this book, can represent psychic archetypes, which must be overcome- such as the alpha male representing the dark side of the mind that must be defeated or in more concrete terms understood as controlled. The white bitch can also represent the internal child or the anima in a man, that must also be defeated or else integrated into the ego correctly to fully individuate, she can also represent sexual desires, while the alpha can represent jealousy and also the masculine side of the man as a whole, where the masculine must come into control, or else excessive animalistic aggression, with a lack of morals and values can ensue.

The black lady at the end, represents 2 things- the fact that there is indeed some innocence left in the world. Also, we should have hope to find that innocence and those who are right for us. More on, it also represents the other side of Sparkles- it represents a closure between the mind- an acceptance of tragedy. It represents understanding oneself- as Carl Jung would say- it represents individuation. It represents how tragedy builds us stronger. Yet it represents the alleviation of evil. For the black lady is she who shall fix his heart.

This book represents how the issues of evil emerge out of toxic environments- this is when a person decides to integrate with the environment and thus become evil- there is another option, which is to be depicted more in my other book, The Existentialist, when one decides not to take the evil route. There is always suffering of the heart- perhaps the worst suffering is the suffering of the heart. Yet one should appreciate how dangerous environments can be- how they change a person and in a case like that of this book- it seems like, perhaps it is impossible to not become evil. It is a scary concept to grasp- the idea of evil and how we are lucky if we don't fall much into evil, for evil seems to be everywhere- a very dangerous concept. But furthermost- it seems our society has become ruptured and broken and thus we always see that evil everywhere. And in all honesty- it seems right to see that evil everywhere. How can we not see the evil everywhere, when evil builds upon evil so often.

The murder does not necessarily need to be seen as a murder, yet it can be viewed as the execution of some sort of action which we personally do, despite our view against it. We don't like that we have done it, yet due to the suffering of our insides, we execute on it. And how often do we partake in such things due to unbearable circumstances of our environment. And the unbearable circumstances of ourselves.

There is no direct answer to explain why the Curt's exist- that is because for a man to become evil is simply too easy in today's society. A man must be very careful to be good, for else, it almost seems that by default he becomes bad. Men are often driven by pleasure- there are far too many hedonistic men, for a man's desire is most outwardly.

Vanity is everywhere! It is simply a sad thing and it destroys society, by concealing reality. It allows the vermillion to spread, for it disguises the vermillion. Often we can simply make something evil seem good with a few twists of the words- that is vanity!

See how the cycle continues- Curts father abandoned him, now a bastard is born- abandoned by his father. The cycle continues with the lonely dog having bastard puppies. Lassie gives up her child for adoption, like she had adopted Sparkles. This is the large problem with society- that there is a reinforcing feedback loop, which sends society further and further down into destruction.

Humans are nurtured to be weak by society. The society nurtures corruption, immaturity and hedonism. The highschool system corrupts kids over lack of morality in contemporary society, especially in the west.

The ego referred to in this story is the psychological ego- a complex center of the mind responsible for identity, and thus it dictates behavior, perceptions and the comprehension of reality. The author believe the ego developed without conscious effort to construct it correctly, leads to it automatically being constructed through external forces- this latter situation is disastrous, for it becomes a prostitute to society- a corrupted society- where it becomes toxified by the exchange of itself for the various means of payment society offers: often vanity. Furthermore, this ego is then shaped into an object lying near the average psychic identity of the local society and because society is broken, so too does the person become broken and this leads further into a reinforcing feedback loop, where each subsequent generation strays further and further away into the darkness- it can be seen why rates of suicides have steadily been increasing in the United states over the last 20 years, from 10.5%(1999) to 22.4%(2019) (Hedegaard et al, 2021).

Finally, Sparkles turns into a human after he has finally experienced curiosity in its fullness in its three parts: the question, the seeking of the question and finally the answers. Then sparkles as a human has the functioning faculty to think and ponder more greatly about the greater depths of psychology and philosophy.

A major issue in today's society is that people think pride is a virtue. I have no idea why? Or what even people have to be proud about. Pride is the ego holding onto things, to overcompensate for insecurity- an almost existential insecurity- for a grand insecurity causes one to lose their concept of reality and thus, a weak character over reaches its identification with certain aspects of themselves in order to cover up the true reality of the human being naked with from anything great in their pure form. When people don't understand how weak a species we are and society is vain, we are spun into a grand uncertainty about the order of ourselves and the universe, thus

we are put into an existential mode: an existential insecurity.
We are really very insignificant in the grand scheme of the
universe and we are taught to believe by society that we must
be significant and thus, when we have the realization of our
insignificance, we are then sent into an existential crisis, which
is tightly mingled with an ego death, for our deep internal
concept of reality is broken- and when our concepts of reality
are broken, we experience existentialism.

It's hope that causes the philosopher dog to once again be
lonely. Hope often makes a person lonely... hope to be loved...
for it is that hope that manifests itself in the wanting for more
than simply oneself and it is exactly this hope which allows the
greatness of such a connection to be formed and it is exactly
this hope which may despair and so form despised labels on,
but above all it is this hope which breeds strength out of the
vast pains or grand pleasures it evokes.
 Simply hope produces desire and desire makes one incontent.
But conversely: no pain no gain. This is also an example of the 2
staged model of contraction and rarefaction- where suffering
(contraction) then allows for pleasure (rarefaction).

224

Bibliographie:

Hedegaard H, Curtin SC, Warner M. Suicide mortality in
the United States, 1999–2019. NCHS Data Brief, no 398.
Hyattsville, MD: National Center for Health Statistics.
2021. DOI: https://dx.doi.org/10.15620/ cdc:101761.

PROTECTION OF WOMEN FROM DOMESTIC VIOLENCE ACT, 2005

A CONCISE COMMENTARY

MUKESH KUMAR SUMAN